TRUE TO LIFE

STARTER

Stephen Slater
Simon Haines

CLASS BOOK

CAMBRIDGE
UNIVERSITY PRESS

PUBLISHED BY THE PRESS SYNDICATE OF THE UNIVERSITY OF CAMBRIDGE
The Pitt Building, Trumpington Street, Cambridge, United Kingdom

CAMBRIDGE UNIVERSITY PRESS
The Edinburgh Building, Cambridge CB2 2RU, UK
40 West 20th Street, New York, NY 10011–4211, USA
10 Stamford Road, Oakleigh, VIC 3166, Australia
Ruiz de Alarcón 13, 28014 Madrid, Spain
Dock House, The Waterfront, Cape Town 8001, South Africa

http://www.cambridge.org

First published 1998
Fifth printing 2001

Printed in the United Kingdom at the University Press, Cambridge

ISBN 0 521 59578 9 Class Book
ISBN 0 521 59577 0 Personal Study Workbook
ISBN 0 521 59576 2 Teacher's Book
ISBN 0 521 59575 4 Class Cassette Set
ISBN 0 521 59574 6 Personal Study Workbook Cassette
ISBN 0 521 59573 8 Personal Study Audio CD

COURSE OVERVIEW

HI AND BYE

Language focus:	Vocabulary:
pronouns: *I, you, he, she, it, we, they*	places
verb *to be*	numbers 1–10
questions: *How are you? Am I late?*	alphabet
introductions: *I'm ..., this is ...*	*Mr, Ms, Mrs*
saying hello and goodbye	adjectives
	Yes/No

A ▎ HELLO, AM I LATE?

1 Hi! | *Hello/Hi, how are you? (I'm) fine, thanks.* |

A 🎧 Listen. Match 1, 2, 3, 4, 5 with a, b, c, d, e.

B 🎧 Listen. Guess the pictures for the greetings.

Greetings
Good morning. I'm Gloria Jones.
Hi, nice day.
Hello, Juan.
Hello, I'm Jill Smith. Are you Kemal Caglar?
Hi, Maria. How are you?

Replies
Hello, Ryoko.
Yes, pleased to meet you.
Hi, Phil, fine thanks.
... morning.
Oh, hi, yes ... beautiful.

C 🎧 Listen. Match greetings and replies.

2 Pleased to meet you | *I, you* |

🎧 Listen to the examples. Make conversations.

Example 1: *Hello, I'm .... Pleased to meet you.*
Hello, pleased to meet you. I'm ....
Example 2: *Hi, how are you?*
Hello, fine thanks, and you?
Fine, thanks.

HELP	In your language?
Pardon?	....

3 Am I late?

Am I/Are You ...? Yes, you are/No, you're not; Mr/Mrs/Ms

 Listen and tick the box.

Is Ms Tanaka:
a man ♂ ☐ a woman ♀ ☒?
late? Yes ☐ No ☐

Is Mr James:
a man ♂ ☐ a woman ♀ ☒?
late? Yes ☐ No ☐

Is Mrs Sukova:
a man ♂ ☐ a woman ♀ ☒?
late? Yes ☐ No ☐

Listen again and complete 1–3.

1. Are you Ms Tanaka?
   Yes, I am.

   .... late?

   ....

   ....

2. Are you Mr James?
   Yes, I am.

   .... late?

   ....

   I'm sorry.

3. Are you Mrs Petrovna?
   No, I'm not, I'm Mrs Irina Sukova.

   .... late?

   ....

   ....

Practise the conversations.

4 Introducing ...

I'm ... and this is ...; What's your name?

> Hello. I'm Jacques Leotard; this is Maria Gasso.

1

> What's your name?

2

> Hi!

3

 Listen to 1, 2 and 3. Write the words.

Ask and answer, like this:

What's your name?

I'm .... and this is ....

HELP	In your language?
first name	....
family name	....

A Complete 1–3.

1. ANDREW: Hi, I'm Andrew.
   JENNIFER: Hello, ... Jennifer.
   ANDREW: Pleased to .... you.

2. What's your name?
   Jacques, and .... is Elsa.
   I'm Peter. Pleased .... meet you.

3. Hi, how .... you?
   Fine, thanks, Santo, and ....?
   Fine, ...

B Complete this:

Short	Long	Question
I'm	I	Am ....?
You're	You are	.... you?
Man	*Woman*	
....	Ms	
	....	

C Write the short forms.

Long	*Short*
I am Alessandre.	.... Alessandre.
What is your name?	.... your name?

D Mark 3 strong sounds in a, and 3 in b.

Example: *Are you **pleased**? **Yes**, I **am**.*

    a. Are you Juan? Yes, I am.
    b. Am I late? No, you're not.

E Correct sentences a and b.

a. How are you? Fine, thank.
b. Are you Maria? Yes, I'm.

B   HOW ARE YOU?

1 How are you? Fine | responding to *How are you?* |

▢▢ Listen to 1, 2, 3 and 4. Is the answer from a man or a woman?

Hello, I'm fine, thanks.

Hello. How are you?

Hello, not bad, thank you.

Hello, I'm OK, thanks.

Hi, all right, thanks.

	Man?	Woman?
1	☐	☐
2	☐	☐
3	☐	☐
4	☐	☐

Practise like this:

Hello, how are you?

(I'm) fine/OK/all right/not bad, thanks/thank you.

2 They're all right

reading; she's, he's, we're, they're, it's

The Bosnic family, from Croatia, is in Australia.
Read a letter to Alex, a friend in London.

Complete 2 and 3.

> Vesna is in Sydney, and she's fine. Goran
> is in Brisbane. He's OK. (Brisbane is a city
> – it's beautiful.)
>   Anna and Nick are in Tokyo, for a meeting.
> They're all right.
>   And Josef and I? We're fine – and the
> coffee shop is fine. It's busy in the morning.
>   How are you, Alex? Are you busy? How
> about a letter from you?
>   It's late! Goodbye for now.
> Write please!
>   Love
>   Eli and Josef

Alex Jones
20 Elmsdale Road
London E17 6PW
Great Britain

1	2	3
Vesna	a woman	She's (she is) fine.
Goran	a man	H............. (he is) OK.
Anna and Nick	a man and a woman	They're (they ....) all right.
Josef and I	a man and a	We.......... (we are) fine.
the coffee shop	a shop	It's (it ....) busy.
Brisbane	a	It.......... (.......... is) beautiful.

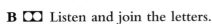 Listen to Alex. Repeat the expressions in 3.

Ask your teacher about people in your class.

Examples: A: *How's Marisa?*   A: *How's Carlos?*   A: *How are Melina and Stavros?*
          B: *She's fine, thanks.*   B: *He's OK.*   B: *They're all right, thanks.*
                                    C: *Good.*   C: *Good.*

3 Is that an *e* or a *c*?

alphabet

A  Listen and repeat the letters.

A B C	D E F	G H I	J K L	M N O	P Q R	S T	U V	W X	Y Z
a b c	d e f	g h i	j k l	m n o	p q r	s t	u v	w x	y z

B Listen and join the letters.

A
BEF
TCDGH
USRQNMI
VWXYPOLKJ
Z
FINISH

A   B

Faithfully yours

William

C What are the letters and names?

Listen and write.

A Look at the names for the meeting. Write *He's a man* or *She's a woman*.

MEMO

Ms E Ahmad ....

Mr G Smith ....

Mrs A Etvos ....

B Answer the questions.

1. How's Goran? .... fine.
2. How's Vesna? .... OK.
3. How are Anna and Nick? .... not bad.
4. How's your teacher? ....
5. How's the meeting? .... all right.

C Look at the letters of the alphabet.

ABCDFGHIJKMNOPQRSTUVXYZ

Three letters are not there.
Write the three letters. ....

C HOW ABOUT A DRINK? OK

1 In conversation

Listen and read.

FRIEND: Hell**o**.
JOHN: **Hi**, is **An**na there?
FRIEND: Just a **min**ute.
ANNA: Hell**o**.
JOHN: **Hi**, **An**na, it's **John**.
ANNA: Oh, **hi**. How are **you**?
JOHN: I'm **fine**. Are you **bus**y?
ANNA: **No**, not **real**ly.
JOHN: **Grea**t ... How about a **cof**fee?
ANNA: Mm, **OK**.

4

?

Answer 1–4.

1. Is Anna there? Yes, she is. ☐ No, she isn't. ☐
2. Is John OK? Yes, he is. ☐ No, he isn't. ☐
3. Is Anna busy? Yes, she is. ☐ No, she isn't. ☐
4. Picture 4 is: a. ☐ b. ☐

a   b

Practise the telephone conversation. Choose questions from the box.

How about a drink?   How about a beer?

How about a coffee?   How about a tea?

---

2 What's your number? numbers 1–10

A ⬚ Listen.

> 10 (ten) 9 (nine) 8 (eight) 7 (seven) 6 (six) 5 (five)
> 4 (four) 3 (three) 2 (two) 1 (one) 0 (zero)

B ⬚ Repeat the numbers.

C ⬚ Listen and complete the telephone numbers:

a 80 _ 25 _ _ _

b 6 _ _ 1 _ _ _ _

c 1 _ _ _ 2 _ _ _

d your telephone number 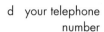 - - - - - - - - - - - - -

Ask two learners: *What's your number?*
Write two telephone numbers.

1. Name .... Number ....
2. Name .... Number ....

HELP	In your language?
66 = double six	....
44 = double four	....
99 = double nine	....
0 = zero	....

3 Thanks for a nice day   goodbye and thank you

⬚ Listen. Write 1, 2, 3 and 4 in the boxes ⬚.

Is it the end of your class? Say goodbye to your teacher.

A Match numbers and words.

6	four
2	seven
8	six
4	five
9	nine
1	three
3	two
10	eight
7	one
5	ten

C Circle Yes or No.

1. You're = You are	Yes/No
2. You're = Your	Yes/No
3. Hi = Hello	Yes/No
4. Goodbye = Bye bye	Yes/No
5. Thank you = Thanks	Yes/No
6. 88 = double five	Yes/No
7. What's ...? = What is ...?	Yes/No

B Rewrite the conversation.

GUY: you how are Hi?
JANE: you fine. busy Are I'm?
GUY: really Not
JANE: drink Good a about how?
GUY: KO Yes

PERSONAL STUDY WORKBOOK

- greetings
- writing a note
- pronunciation of final sounds
- visual dictionary – letters and numbers 1–10
- reading – episode 1 of *Lost in time*

D CLASSROOM ENGLISH

1 Classroom English   questions with *can*

Listen and tick 7 boxes.

2 Practise classroom language in English listening for *can* questions

A 🔲 Listen and answer questions 1–4.

1.
2. ....
3. ....
4.

B 🔲 Listen to 1 and 4 again. Check your answers.

With a partner, ask and answer questions about:

busy	late	fine	m<u>ee</u>ting (double *e*)	park	co<u>ff</u><u>ee</u> (double *f*, double *e*)
beer	city	tea			

Can you spell ....? Can you write ....?
(in English)

3 What's 'ejemplo' in English? classroom questions with *what*

Complete.

Word in English	*question (?)*	*example*	*tick (✔)*	*check*	*answer*
In your language	....	....	....	....	....

🔲 Listen. Ask and answer, like this:

1.
   A: What's 'example' in (Spanish)?
   B: Ejemplo.
   A: Thank you.

2.
   A: What's 'pregunta' in English?
   B: Question.
   A: Thanks.

WELCOME!

Language focus:
What's this/that? It's a/the
this is / that is (that's)
Is it …? Yes, it is / No, it isn't.
Where's …?
prepositions of place: *in, from, on, at*
possessive adjectives: *my, your*
plural nouns

Vocabulary:
numbers 11–30
first – tenth
places: countries, cities, buildings, hotels

A COUNTRIES AND CITIES

1 Welcome   listening and speaking

Listen and match numbers 1, 2, 3, 4 with pictures A, B, C, D.

A Rome

B Rio

C Istanbul

D Moscow

Write the name of a country and two cities in this country.

Example: *USA: New York / Los Angeles*

2 Conversation   speaking

Partner A: You are a tourist guide. Welcome a visitor to one of your cities from Exercise 1.

Partner B: You are a visitor. Say thank you and say who you are.

Make a conversation like this:

Example: A: *Hello/Hi, I'm …… Welcome to ……*   B: *Thanks. I'm pleased to be here. I'm ……*

Now B is the guide and A is the visitor.

3 Look! | listening; *Is that …? What's that?* |

Paul and Sue are in a taxi in New York. They are visitors.

Restaurant

Penn
Station

Central Park

The Plaza Hotel

The Statue of Liberty

The World
Trade Centre

A New
York taxi

What do they see? Listen. Find the photos and the names.

Point to the photos and make conversations like this:

A: *What's that?*   B: *It's the Statue of Liberty.*

Now point to the photos and make conversations, like this:

A: *Is that a restaurant?*   B: *No, it isn't. It's a station.*

4 Capital cities | *Where's …? It's in … Yes, it is. No, it isn't.* |

A Match the capital cities with the countries.

Capital cities		*Countries*	
Ankara	Moscow	Japan	Egypt
Cairo	Athens	Greece	Russia
Tokyo	Warsaw	Turkey	Poland

Listen and check your answers.

B Now listen and repeat.

Think of more cities and countries. With a partner ask and answer questions, like this:

A: *Where's Rio?*   B: *It's in Brazil.*

Now ask and answer questions, like this:

A: *Is Istanbul in Turkey?*   B: *Yes, it is.*
A: *Is New York in England?*   B: *No, it isn't.*

HELP	In your language?
I don't know	....

✔ Quick Check

A Finish the conversations.

1. a: Hello, I'...... John. Welcome .... Rio.
   b: Thanks. It's good to .... here.
2. a: Where .... they?
   b: They're .... Moscow.
3. a: ....'s that?
   b: ....'s a station.
4. a: .... that the Empire State Building?
   b: No, it ....

B Correct these sentences.

1. My name Paul.
2. Cairo is Egypt.
3. A: Is the Statue Liberty in Ankara?
   B: No, it is.
4. A: Are London in France?
   B: Yes, it isn't.
5. Hello. Welcome Rome.

B NUMBERS AND ADDRESSES

1 Ten plus `numbers 11–30`

A 🔊 Choose five of the numbers 11–30. Listen for your numbers.

B 🔊 Now read, listen and repeat the numbers 11–30.

eleven	twelve	thirteen	fourteen	fifteen	sixteen	seventeen	eighteen
nineteen	twenty	twenty-one	twenty-two	twenty-three	twenty-four		
twenty-five	twenty-six	twenty-seven	twenty-eight	twenty-nine	thirty		

C 🔊 Look at these pictures. Say the numbers. Listen and find the numbers in the pictures.

🔊 Listen again and write the numbers. Which numbers are not in the picture?

2 What's your address? `listening; numbers`

🔊 Listen to some conversations at the Royal Hotel. Write the numbers and names.

What's your address, please, Mr Jones?

It's 25, York Avenue, Liverpool, L14 2PR.

FAMILY NAME	FIRST NAME	ADDRESS
1 Jones	Peter	.........., York Avenue, Liverpool, L .... PR
2 Smith	....	.........., Exeter Gardens, Manchester, M .... AG
3 Procter	....	.........., New Road, Melbourne .... Australia
4 Harriman	Dorothy	.........., Central Avenue, Washington DC, USA
5 Collins	Angela	.........., Barrack Street, Cape Town, ... South Africa
6 Charles	....	.............., Park Road, Perth .... Western Australia

Write the names and addresses of three other learners. Ask: *What's your address?*

3 Where's my room? `listening; numbers`

A  You are in a hotel lift. Listen and repeat the numbers of the floors.

Match the words with the numbers.

eight	1	fourth
five	2	tenth
four	3	second
nine	4	sixth
one	5	eighth
seven	6	fifth
six	7	third
ten	8	seventh
three	9	first
two	10	ninth

B ▭ Listen to more conversations. Write the numbers of the rooms and the floors.

	Room	*Floor*
a. Mrs Smith	....	....
b. Mr Procter	....	....
c. Ms Harriman	....	....
d. Miss Collins	....	....
e. Mr Charles	....	....

HELP	In your language?
family name	....
first name	....
Here's (is)	....
That's right.	....

Choose a floor and room at the hotel. Make conversations like this:

A: *Where's your room?*   B: *I'm in Room 657. It's on the sixth floor.*

4 Where's the restaurant? `reading; speaking`

These are places in a hotel. Match the words and the pictures.

Bar	Coffee bar	Conference room	Disco	Gym
Restaurant	Rest room	Sauna	Swimming pool	

Where are these places? Decide and write the floor number.

Example: Restaurant – *fourth*

Make conversations in pairs, like this:

A: *Excuse me. Where's the restaurant?*   B: *It's on the fourth floor.*   A: *Thanks a lot.*

✓ Quick Check

A Write the questions for these answers.

1. My first name's Pete.
2. My family name's Bogart.
3. It's 23, Pool Road, London.
4. It's 0171 234 8351.

B Correct the mistakes.

1. What your address?
2. My room's on fourth floor.
3. You're on Room 591. Here your key.
4. Is my room in the first floor?
5. That's your telephone number, please?

C AT THE HOTEL

1 Enquiries   listening and speaking; *Can I have?*

A 🎧 Listen and read.

CLARE: Hello. Room Service. This is Clare.
CARTER: Hello, Mr Carter here. Room 504.
CLARE: How can I help?
CARTER: Can I have a beer, please?
CLARE: Of course, Mr Carter.

🎧 Listen again and repeat.

Now make conversations in pairs. Take turns.

Partner A: You are Room Service.
Partner B: You are a hotel guest.
Ask for a drink.

B 🎧 Listen and read this conversation.

MATTHEW: Hello, Reception. Matthew here.
BOUTON: Hi, this is Room 613. This is Miss Bouton.
MATTHEW: How can I help?
BOUTON: Where's the gym, please?
MATTHEW: It's on the first floor, Miss Bouton.
BOUTON: Thank you.
MATTHEW: You're welcome.

🎧 Listen again and repeat.

Make conversations. Take turns.

Partner A: You are Reception.
Partner B: You are a hotel guest.
Ask where a place is in the hotel.

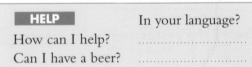

HELP	In your language?
How can I help?	....
Can I have a beer?	....

2 Hi from Brussels   reading and writing

Read the e-mail. Who is it from? Who is it to?

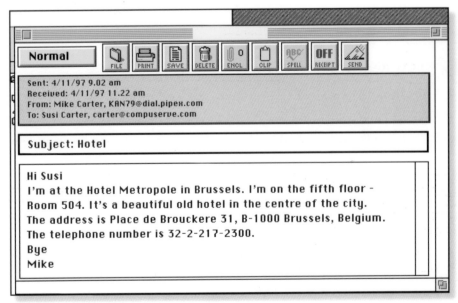

Normal   FILE PRINT SAVE DELETE ENCL CLIP SPELL RECEIPT SEND

Sent: 4/11/97 9.02 am
Received: 4/11/97 11.22 am
From: Mike Carter, KAN79@dial.pipex.com
To: Susi Carter, carter@compuserve.com

Subject: Hotel

Hi Susi
I'm at the Hotel Metropole in Brussels. I'm on the fifth floor –
Room 504. It's a beautiful old hotel in the centre of the city.
The address is Place de Brouckere 31, B-1000 Brussels, Belgium.
The telephone number is 32-2-217-2300.
Bye
Mike

modern

old

You are in a hotel in a city in another country. Write an e-mail to a friend.

3 In conversation

📼 Listen and read these conversations.

1. A: Excuse me. Is this your key?
   B: Yes, it is. Thanks very much.
2. A: Excuse me. Is this your key?
   B: No, it isn't. I'm in Room 27.
3. A: Excuse me. Is this the third floor?
   B: Yes, it is.
4. A: Excuse me. Is this the tenth floor?
   B: No, it isn't. It's the ninth floor.

Make your own conversations in pairs.

✔ Quick Check

A Rewrite the conversation.

A: Hello. is this in Reception Hannah.
B: in 504 Room Ms Spiller this is. Hello.
A: I can help how?
B: please a coffee I can have?
A: Ms Spiller certainly.

B Fill the gaps in the e-mail with one of these words:

at   from   in   of   on   to

```
................    Jan Luff, luff@compuserve.com
................    Paul James, KAN23@dial.pipex.com

Hi, Jan
I'm ........................ the Embajada ........................ Madrid.
I'm ........................ the sixth floor ........................ the hotel.
I'm ........................ Room 615. It's a beautiful old hotel
........................ the centre ........................ the city.

Bye, Paul
```

C Continue the numbers. Write the words.

1. five   seven   nine   ....
2. twenty-two twenty-one twenty   ....
3. three   six   nine   ....
4. four   nine   sixteen   ....
5. tenth   ninth   eighth   ....

PERSONAL STUDY WORKBOOK
- vocabulary of countries, cities and buildings
- listening to conversations between hotel guests and staff
- reading and writing e-mails
- pronunciation work
- visual dictionary – countries of the world
- reading – episode 2 of *Lost in time*

REVIEW OF UNIT 1

1 How do you spell that? | alphabet |

Write five English words.   Example: *morning coffee meet ...*

Choose one word.   Example: *meet*

Ask your partner: *How do you spell 'meet'?*

2 Matching | questions and answers |

Match the questions with the answers.

Questions	Answers
1. Are you Hitomi?	Fine, thanks.
2. What's your name?	Yes, OK.
3. How are you?	No, she isn't.
4. Is Julia in?	She's OK.
5. How's Renate?	Frederic Paris.
6. How about a coffee?	Yes, I am.

3 Words | vocabulary |

Write three words with double letters.

Example: *meet*

Write three words ending in *y*.

Example: *real**ly***

Write the opposites.

Example: good – *bad*

1. Yes – ....   4. Hi – ....

2. question – ....   5. is – ....

3. Hello – ....

Find five groups of three words.

beer	day	eight	fine	Good morning	coffee	Hello	minute
morning	nice	Hi	pleased	six	tea	two	

Examples: *eight, six,* ....

....   *coffee,* ...., ...

Choose the word with a different sound.

Example: *he   she   Hi   meet* – <u>Hi</u>

1. eight   Hi   nice   fine   – ....   4. am   park   bad   thank   – ....

2. shop   so   not   on   – ....   5. great   day   eight   right   – ....

3. no   so   two   hello   – ....

3

PEOPLE AND THINGS IN MY LIFE

Language focus:
possessive adjectives
Who is this/that?
Where ... from?
questions about age (*How old is ...?*)
questions (*to be*)
short answer forms
there is/are
saying thank you/responding

Vocabulary:
numbers 31–100
describing people
personal possessions

A   FRIENDS IN PHOTOGRAPHS

1   Is your manager nice? | *your; describing people; Yes, ... is/are; No, ... isn't/aren't* |

Write the words from the box in 1, 2, 3, 4 and 5.

| friend   colleague   husband   manager   wife |

Our teachers

Mr J Abbott, MA, CELTA
Mrs S Best, BA, DELTA
Mr A Clark, MA, MBA
Ms M Donovan, MA, DELTA

Listen to the questions. Write the answers.

Questions	Answers
1. Is your wife busy?	....
2. Is your manager popular?	....
3. Are your friends nice?	....
4. Are your colleagues nice?	....

HELP   In your language?
best friend   ....

Ask two of the questions in groups.

2 Who's this?

How old is …?; numbers 20–60; Who's this/that?; my, your, his, her, our, their

Ask and answer questions about the photos, like this:

Examples: *How old is he? About twenty (20)./Twentyish./About thirty (30)./Thirtyish.*
How old is she? About forty (40)./Fortyish.
How old are they? About fifty (50)./Fiftyish./About sixty (60)./Sixtyish.

Listen. Label the photos 1, 2, 3 or 4.

Read a–f. Listen again. Match a–f with photos 1–4.

a: … and *her* husband Michael.   Photo number 1   d: She's *your* manager?   Photo number 2
b: They're *our* friends.   Photo number 2   e: … that's *their* guide.   Photo number 4
c: That's *my* manager – Maria.   Photo number 2   f: That's *his* wife.   Photo number 3

Talk about pictures or photos, like this:

This is …
Who's that? He's/She's …
Who are they? They're …

3 Money or books?

numbers 31–100

Listen to the numbers. Match the numbers and pictures.

Numbers										Which picture?
1. 31	32	33	34	35	36	37	38	39	40	…………
2. 41	42	43	44	45	46	47	48	49	50	
51	52	53	54	55	56	57	58	59	60	…………
3. 61	62	63	64	65	66	67	68	69	70	…………
4. 71	72	73	74	75	76	77	78	79	80	
81	82	83	84	85	86	87	88	89	90	
91	92	93	94	95	96	97	98	99	100	…………

A   B   C   D

Practise counting.

✔ Quick Check

A Write the missing pronouns.

1. Is he OK?
   Mm, ...'s fine!
2. Is .... all right?
   Yes, she's OK.
3. Are they busy?
   No, ... aren't.
4. Are .... OK?
   Mm, I'm fine, thanks.

B Correct the sentences.

1. You house is very nice.
2. They're house is interesting.
3. Her husband is in he's coffee shop.
4. Oh, you are her wife.
5. Who are their?
6. They are her friend.

C Tick Yes or No.

		Yes	No
1.	Who's = Who is	☐	☐
2.	They're = Their	☐	☐
3.	Your = You are	☐	☐
4.	You're = You are	☐	☐
5.	His = He's	☐	☐
6.	His = He's	☐	☐
7.	About sixty = 50	☐	☐
8.	Fortyish = 40 + or − 2	☐	☐

D Complete the table.

I	my	we	....
you	....	they	....
it	its		
she	her		
....	his		

E Write 1–5 under *man*, *woman* or *man* or *woman*.

1 friend   2 wife   3 manager
4 husband   5 colleague

B   RINGS AND ROOMS

1   This ring is 50 years old | personal possessions; pronoun *it*; adjectives |

Look at this photo. Is it a man or a woman?

watch

ring

 Listen. Match the speakers and the pictures.

A    B    C

earrings

Write: *old*, *new*, *small*, *big*, *special*.

Ask and answer questions in your classroom.

Examples: *Is that a new ring? Yes, it is./No, it isn't.*
            Is that a special watch? Yes, it's very special.
            Are they old earrings? No, they're new, from my husband.

---

2 Where's it from?

Where ... from? questions; countries/nationalities; dual listening

Guess. Where's A from? Is it from Spain? (Is it Spanish?) And B, C?

Turkey – Turkish
Spain – Spanish
Japan – Japanese
China – Chinese
Ireland – Irish

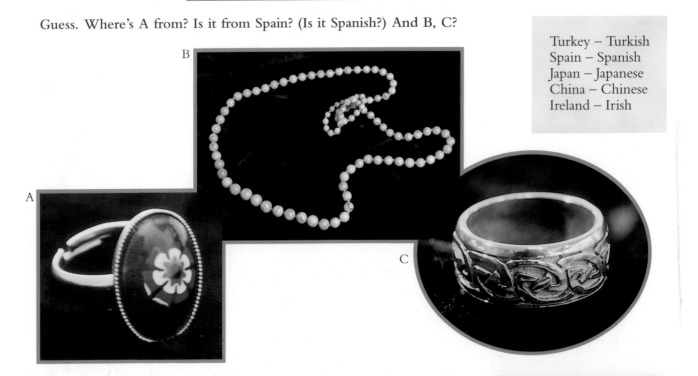

⬚⬚ ⬚⬚ Listen. Write the 3 countries or the nationalities.

Ask questions about these things, like this:

Where's the ring from?
Where are the earrings from?
Is the ring Indian?

The answers are on page 111.

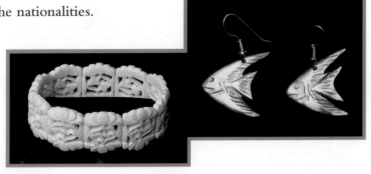

3 Twenty rings and one mobile phone

vocabulary; plurals; there is/are

Guess the number of things in your group.

Things	Number in your group
ring	....
key	....
watch	....
mobile phone	....
business card	....
(Your word)	....

HELP   In your language?
There are no mobile phones. ....

Complete sentences like this:

*There's (There is) 1 mobile phone. There are **20** rings. There are **12** watches.*

4 Things on the floor

Look at the picture and read the text.

Things on the floor!

There are one or two things on the floor of our bedroom. There's a key, a letter (from my manager!) and there are two books, and, oh yes, under the bed there's an earring (so that's where it is!), an old business card (with the name Ms. Maria Suarez, Manager, Capital Disco) a magazine (called Ideal Homes), a phone book and a cat!!
But there isn't a cat in our flat!

phone book

magazine

cat

floor

Circle true or false. (T/F)

1. There's a key under the bed. T/F
2. There is an earring under the bed. T/F
3. The letter is to the manager. T/F
4. The cat isn't under the bed. T/F

HELP	In your language?
There's nothing on our floor.	....

Write *a* or *an*.

.... phone book   .... key   .... earring   .... letter
.... bedroom   .... business card   .... cat

Talk about things on the floor of your office, car or bedroom. Use a dictionary.

A Match A and B.

A	B
an earring	he
a wife	they
colleagues	it
a husband	it
a key	she

And your teacher? ....

B Put these under *a thing, a place* or *a person*.

a mobile phone   a park
a friend   a ring   a woman
a room   a letter   a classroom
a business card   a husband

C Complete the questions.

1. A: ....
    Italy?
    B: No, it's from France.
2. A: This is nice.
    B: Thanks.
    A: Is ....
    Greece?
    B: Yes, from Corfu.

C   IT'S OUR CAR, THANK YOU

1 Is that our car? | reading and speaking; practice with *we/our* |

A

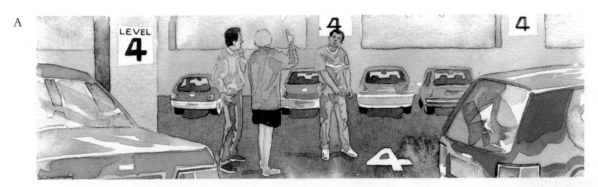

B

C

Read the conversations and put the correct numbers under the pictures.

1. A: Is that our car?
   B: I'm not sure.

2. A: Are you lost?
   B: Yes, I think we are.

3. A: This is the fourth level.
   B: Is it? Our car's on the fifth level.

▭▭ Listen and check your answer. Practise the conversations.

2 Cars   `speaking practice with adjectives`

Ask and answer questions about your car or one of the photos. Use words in this box.

Old   NEW   BIg   small   our   my   nice

Questions	Answers
Is your car ...?	No, it's ...
	No, our car's ...
	Yes, it is. / No, it isn't.

HELP
It's quite new/old.
We haven't got a car.

In your language?
....
....

3 In conversation   `saying thank you and responding`

🎧 Listen. Match the pictures with 1, 2 and 3.

1. A: Are you OK now?
   B: Yeah, fine. Thanks for your help.
   A: Don't mention it. You're welcome any time.

2. A: Thank you very much for the information.
   B: You're very welcome.

3. A: Here's your drink.
   B: Thanks a lot.

A

B

C

Partner A: Say *thanks* or *thank you*
for one or two things.
Partner B: Respond.

4 Thank you very much for the ...

Write a 'thank you' note to a friend for one of the things.

flowers   earrings   book

Say: *They're/it's nice/beautiful/fantastic/great.*

Dear _____

Thank you _____

_____ for the

_____ . It's/They're

_____ .

Best wishes

_____

✔ Quick Check

A Put a tick if 1 to 3 mean the same. Put a cross if they are different.

1. thank you very much = thanks a lot
2. small = big
3. our car's = our cars

B Match A and B.

A	B
I	our
she	their
it	his
you	my
he	its
they	her
we	your

C Are they places or things? Write the words in 2 lists.

car park   watch   office   bedroom
earring   car   key

Places   *Things* ✏

PERSONAL STUDY WORKBOOK

- possessive adjective practice
- question intonation
- writing about a friend
- visual dictionary – personal things
- reading – episode 3 of *Lost in time*

D REVIEW AND DEVELOPMENT

REVIEW OF UNIT 1

1 Same or different? | alphabet pronunciation |

Say the letters in 1, 2 and 3. Which letter sounds different?

1. B C E J T
2. J K P
3. I A Y

📼 Listen and check.

2 Same sounds? | vowel sounds in words |

Say the words. Which vowel sound is different?

1. Hi   fine   nice   bye   day   I'm   nine
2. eight   day   name   am   great

📼 Listen and check.

3 What's good ...? How's she ...? | pronunciation final /s/, /z/ |

In pairs, say the questions and answers. Is the *s* in *How's* and the *s* in *What's* the same sound?

Question	Answer
How's he today?	He's fine.
How's she today?	She's fine.
What's nice at the coffee bar?	The coffee.
What's good at the restaurant?	The tea.

📼 Listen and check.

REVIEW OF UNIT 2

1 Quick quiz | yes, it is/no, it isn't; listening |

A 📼 Listen and answer the six questions with *Yes, it is* or *No, it isn't* in 30 seconds!

B 📼 Listen to the answers.

2 E-mail address | writing |

A 📼 Listen and correct the e-mail addresses.

1. maria.suarez@virtual.net.cum.br
2. angela.collins@Samex.demon.co.uk

B 📼 Listen and write the e-mail address on the business card.

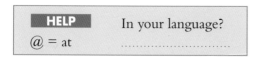

HELP	In your language?
@ = at	....

MAGRIC International

John Smythe
International Marketing Manager

12 Linden Street
Burnside
South Australia 5027
Australia
Telephone (61) 88339 5812
Fax (61) 88339 57444
E-mail _____ @ _____

4

ABOUT TOWN

Language focus:
Is there ...? / Are there (any) ...?
uncertainty: *perhaps / I think*
showing interest: *Really? / Is it really? / That's interesting*
talking about age: *How old is it?*

Vocabulary:
numbers over 100
buildings in towns
north, south, east, west

A TOWNS

1 Public buildings [*perhaps/I think; vocabulary*]

Match these town words with the symbols.

bank   cinema   library   nightclub   police station
post office   sports centre   theatre

Look at the picture of a Roman town. Where are these buildings?
You decide. Talk to your partner like this:

A: *What's this?*   B: *It's a library./Perhaps it's a bank./I think it's a theatre.*

HELP	In your language?
Perhaps	....
I think	....

2 Home towns [listening]

Satoshi (Japan), Raymundo (Mexico) and Paloma (Spain) are answering
questions about their home towns. Listen and tick (✓) or cross (✗) the boxes.

	cinema	*nightclub*	*sports centre*	*theatre*
Satoshi	☐	☐	☐	☐
Raymundo	☐	☐	☐	☐
Paloma	☐	☐	☐	☐

3 Another town   is there?/are there?; speaking

Think about a town you know well. Write numbers in the table.

	sports centre	cinema	nightclub	theatre
Example:	0	3	1	1
You	....	....	....	....
1.	....	....	....	....
2.	....	....	....	....

Ask two people about their towns. Make conversations like this:

A: *Is there a sports centre in your town?*   B: *Yes, there is./No, there isn't.*
A: *Are there any cinemas?*   B: *Yes, there are./No, there aren't.*

Now talk about other places. For example, banks, libraries or discos.

Statement:	Question:	Short answer:
There is/There's a cinema in my town.	**Is there a** cinema in your town?	Yes, **there is.**/No, **there isn't.**
There are six banks in my town.	**Are there any** banks in your town?	Yes, **there are.**/No, **there aren't.**

4 Your dream town   reading; writing

Read about a real town.

My town is small.
There are two banks,
a police station and a
cinema, but there isn't
a sports centre. There's
a hotel and six or seven
shops, but there aren't
any nightclubs.

Write about your dream town.

✔ Quick Check

A Match the questions and the answers.
Sometimes there are two answers.

Questions
1. Is there a cinema in your town?
2. Are there any nightclubs in your town?
3. Can I ask you about your town?
4. What about a cinema?

Answers
a. No, there aren't.   d. No, there isn't.
b. Yes, there is.   e. Yes, there are.
c. There are two.   f. Yes, OK.

B Fill in the missing words.

1. There ...*are*.... three nightclubs in my town.
2. A: .....*Is*...... there a library?
   B: .....*No*....., there isn't.

3. A: Are there .... hotels in your town?
   B: Yes, there .... about three or four.
4. There's a theatre, ... there isn't a cinema.
5. A: Is there a police station?
   B: Yes, ...

C Fill in the gaps with a singular or a plural word.

Example: *a cinema two* **cinemas**............

1. a bank   four *banks*......
2. a *nightclub*   five nightclubs..
3. a library   two *labraries*
4. an office   fifteen *offices*......
5. a *city*.....   four cities

1 Hundreds and thousands

numbers 100–10,000

▭▭ ▭▭ Listen and match the numbers on the recording with the pictures.

	Recording	Picture
Example:	1	*B*
	2	....
	3	....
	4	....
	5	....
	6	....
	7	....
	8	....

▭▭ Listen again and repeat the numbers.

Write your own large numbers and say them with another learner.

2 How old is it?

How old? speaking

Match the buildings with the captions.

The Sydney Opera House ☐
The theatre at Epidaurus ☐
The Bank of England ☐
The Great Wall of China ☐
Chartres Cathedral ☐
Topkapı Palace ☐

How old are the buildings? Make guesses like this.

A: *How old is the Great Wall of China?*
B: *I think it's about three thousand years old.*

HELP	In your language?
over 800 years old	....

▭▭ Listen and check your guesses. Write the missing numbers.

1. Topkapı Palace is over .... years old.
2. The theatre at Epidaurus in Greece is over .... years old.
3. The Sydney Opera House is about .... years old.
4. Chartres Cathedral in France is over .... years old.
5. The Bank of England is about .... years old.
6. The Great Wall of China is over .... years old.

3 Your town ┌─────────────────────┐
└─ speaking and writing ─┘

Talk about the ages of places in your town. For example, an old theatre, a modern cinema, a new sports centre.

Write a postcard to a friend. Tell your friend about your town. Use these words or your own words.

1. town/city
2. big/small/old/modern
3. old/new
4. theatre/cathedral/city walls
5. about/over
6., 7., 8.?

Dear Pavlo,
This is my (1) ....
It's very (2) ....
There are some beautiful
(3) .... buildings.
The (4) .... is/are
(5) .... (6)
.... years old and
the (7) .... is about
(8) .... years old.

Best wishes
....

mosque

bridge   castle   church

✔ Quick Check

A Write the words.

1. 101 ....
2. 365 ....
3. 999 ....
4. 1,104 ....
5. 1,500 ....

B Write the numbers.

1. nine thousand eight hundred and seventy-six
2. four thousand six hundred and twenty-seven
3. one thousand one hundred and eleven
4. seven hundred and thirteen
5. two hundred and two

C Find 7 mistakes in the conversation.

A: How old are your town?
B: The theatre is over hundred years old.
A: Is that your a house?
B: No, she isn't.
A: How old it is?
B: Is about 30 years.
A: It very big.

D Match the questions and answers.

1. What's this?
2. How old is it?
3. Is it in Turkey?
4. Is this a cinema?
5. Is it very old?

a. No, it's in England.
b. No, it's only about 30 years old.
c. It's a library.
d. It's over 800 years old.
e. Yes, it is.

1   Geography   vocabulary

Look at this map and make sentences about Edinburgh, London, Cardiff and Belfast.

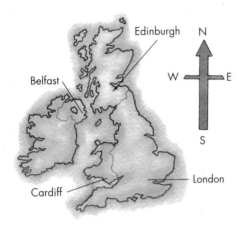

Edinburgh		in	the south		England
London	is		the north	of	Scotland
Cardiff			the east		Britain
Belfast			the west		Northern Ireland
		the	capital		Wales

What do you know about Edinburgh? Talk to a partner.
Read about Edinburgh and check your ideas.

EDINBURGH is the capital of Scotland. It is a big city in the south of the country with about 450,000 people. There is a famous castle and a very old university. Every year there is an important theatre and music festival in Edinburgh.

Edinburgh Castle

Edinburgh Festival

2   Where's the castle?   listening; speaking

Listen to the conversations. Find the places on the map.

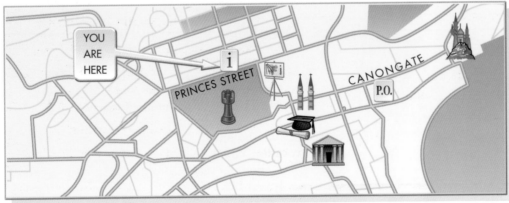

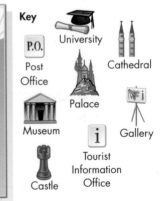

Key

P.O. Post Office

University

Cathedral

Palace

Museum

i Tourist Information Office

Gallery

Castle

Work in pairs. Ask about more places in Edinburgh. Make conversations, like this:

A: *Excuse me, where's the castle?*
B: *It's near the cathedral.*
A: *Thanks very much.*
B: *You're welcome.*

Ask your partner about places in one of these:

– his or her home town or city;
– the capital city of her or his country;

– another town or city she or he knows well;
– a famous old town or city in her or his country.

3 In conversation

showing interest

A 🎧 Listen and read. Match the right photograph.

1. A: Here are my holiday photos.
   B: Thanks. Where's this?
   A: It's Dublin.
   B: Is it a big city?
   A: Yes, it is, there are over a million people.
   B: Really? That's very big.

2. A: And that's St Patrick's Cathedral.
   B: How old is it?
   A: It's about eight hundred years old.
   B: Is it really?

3. A: This is a good photo.
   B: Is it a castle?
   A: Yes, it's Dublin Castle.
   B: Is it very old?
   A: No, it's only about two hundred years old.
   B: That's interesting.

A

B

C

B 🎧 Listen again. A is on the cassette. You are B. Say B's words.

Do this role play.

Partner A: Tell another person about a place in your town.

Partner B: Answer with *Really?/Is it really?/That's interesting*.

Change roles.

✔ Quick Check

A   Fill in the missing words.

1. A: .... the cathedral?
   B: .... in Queen Street.
   A: Thanks .... much.
   B: .... welcome.

2. A: Can I .... you?
   B: Yes. .... there a bank near ....?
   A: Yes, ... one near the tourist office.

3. A: Here's a photo of my university.
   B: How .... is it?
   A: It's about 600 .... old.
   B: Is .... really?

B Write one of these words in the gaps.

in   near   of

1. Milan is .... the north .... Italy.
2. The castle is .... the cathedral.
3. There's a bank .... Oxford Street.
4. This is a photograph .... my house.
5. London is .... the south .... England.

C Put these words into five groups of three.

castle   cathedral   city   country   east   famous
hundred   important   interesting   million
north   south   theatre   thousand   town

Here are the first words in each group:

1. castle   2. city   3. east   4. famous   5. hundred

PERSONAL STUDY WORKBOOK

- vocabulary of towns and public buildings
- a listening exercise about how old places are
- a reading text about Edinburgh
- asking and saying where places in a town are
- pronunciation work
- visual dictionary – the city
- reading – episode 4 of *Lost in time*

REVIEW OF UNIT 2

1　Postcards　| reading; writing |

This is a holiday postcard to a good friend.
Fill in the gaps.

Now write the address of your friend on
the postcard.

Hi ....,
How .... you? I'm ....
France. My hotel .... in
the centre .... Paris. It's
.... beautiful city.
My room is .... the second
floor.
......'.. small but it's .... nice.

See you soon.
Bye.

2　Offices　| numbers; speaking |

Where are these places in the office? Write the floors and
the room numbers in the gaps. Don't show other people!

Restaurant	.... floor	Room ....
Conference room	.... floor	Room ....
Computer room	.... floor	Room ....
Manager's office	.... floor	Room ....
Coffee bar	.... floor	Room ....

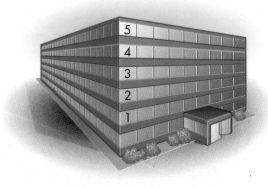

Ask your partner questions about his or her office.

Example:　A: *Is the conference room on the first floor?*　B: *No, it isn't. It's on the second floor.*
　　　　　　A: *What number is it?*　B: *It's number 207.*
Now write about a building you know well. For example:

– an office;　– a big shop;　– a school or college.

REVIEW OF UNIT 3

1　My wife is Japanese　| my, his, her, its, our, their |

Write *my*, *her*, *his*, *its*, *our*, *your* or *their* in the spaces.

1. They are American and .... car is American.
2. We are Spanish, and .... colleagues are Spanish.
3. Our cat is nice, and .... name is Tiddles.

4. Maria is twentyish and .... husband is sixty.
5. I'm married and .... wife is Japanese.
6. Juan is nice and .... wife, Almudena, is great.

2　Friends and colleagues　| his, her, my, their; speaking |

Write the names:

1. a colleague　　　....................
　 his/her wife/husband　....................
　 Their flat/house is in　............ (place)

2. a friend　　　....................
　 his/her wife/husband　....................
　 Their flat/house is in　............ (place)

Talk in groups, like this:
A: *My friend, Jacques, is nice. His wife, Alice, is English. Their flat is in* ....
　　What about your friend?
B: *My friend, Britte, is great. Her husband, Jurgen, is an interesting man. Their house is in*

....

I'VE GOT ONE ON THE WALL

Language focus:	Vocabulary:
has/have got; What have you got?	rooms and things on walls
some/any	people in family
How many ...? Where ...?	colours
	see you expressions

A ROOMS AND THINGS ON THE WALLS

1 It's got a beautiful kitchen | *it's (it has) got; rooms in a home* |

Look at the pictures and read the texts.

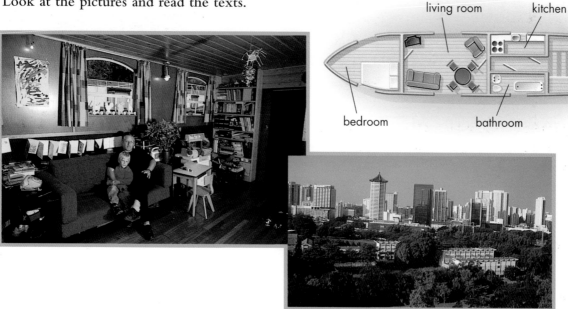

living room   kitchen

bedroom   bathroom

JIM: My home is a boat. Its name is *Dora*.
It's 80 years old. It's got a beautiful kitchen and a nice living room.
There's a bedroom and there's a small bathroom. It's great.

LILY: My home is an apartment. It's on the tenth floor. It's got a modern kitchen and a living room. It's got two bedrooms and a bathroom. The view is beautiful!

Complete the lists of rooms.

The apartment has got a bathroom, ..., ... and a ....
The boat has got ...., ..., ... and ....

Write about your home, like this:

My home is in .... It's got .... and ....
There are .... and it's got a .... The view is ....

HELP	In your language?
toilet	....
big	....

Lesson A ROOMS AND THINGS ON THE WALLS   35

2 On the walls

vocabulary: things in rooms; *have got*; dual listening

▭ ▭ Listen. Tick the things they name. One thing is in the picture but not in the recording. What is it?

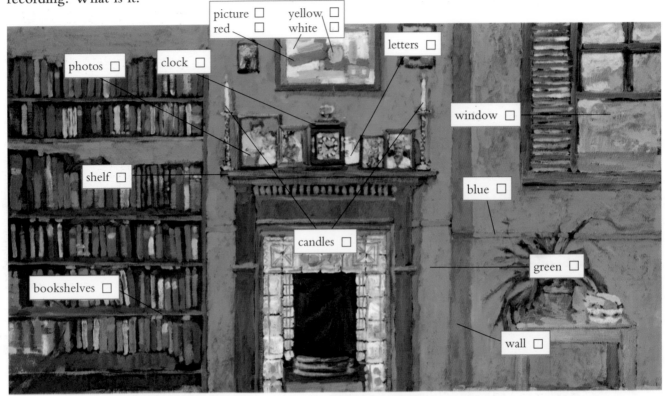

picture ☐ yellow ☐
red ☐ white ☐

letters ☐

photos ☐ clock ☐

window ☐

shelf ☐

blue ☐

candles ☐

green ☐

bookshelves ☐

wall ☐

3 Our living room

question and answer speaking practice with *have got*

▭ Look at these questions and answers. Listen and complete the questions and answers 1 to 7.

Questions

What have you got on the walls of your (1) ....?

Have you got any (2) .... ?

Where are they?

How many (4) .... have you got?

Where are your (5) .... from?

What colour is your (6) .... ?

Answers

We've got lots of things.

Yes, we have.

They're on a (3) ....

We've got lots.

They're Japanese.

It's (7) ....

In small groups, have a conversation about rooms.

HELP	In your language?
a few	....
We haven't got any	....

4 Exchange information

reporting with *she's/he's got ...*

Change groups. Talk about the rooms, like this:

Helena's got (Helena and her husband have got) lots of ... in her (their) living room.
      She's got (They've got) a ...
Her (Their) living room is ...

Remember to comment, like this:

Really? That's interesting!

HELP	In your language?
It sounds nice/interesting	....

A Write the words in the box under *colour* or *on the wall*.

green   picture   yellow   shelf   blue   photo   clock

B Complete the words in the questions and answers.

Questions
Ha _ e you g _ t a _ y pictures?
What col _ _ rs h _ ve y _ u g _ t?
H _ w ma _ y h _ v _ yo _ go _ ?
Ha _ he _ ot an _ clo _ k _?

Answers
Yes, I hav _ .
R _ d a _ d gre _ n.
O _ e or tw _ .
Yes, _ _ has.

C Write in the short form or long form.

Short form
I've got a window.
....

It's fine, thanks.
....

There's a photo on the wall.

Long form
....
I am here today.
....
What is this?
....

D Write the colours of this carpet from Tunisia.

B **BIG FAMILIES?**

1 Always young   vocabulary of the family

She's his mother.
How old is her son? Guess.

He's her brother.
How old is his sister? Guess.

Label the members of the family with the words in the box.

daughter   son
mother   husband
father   sister
wife

brother

2 How big is their family?   `listening; hasn't/haven't got`

📟 Listen and write the numbers of brothers and sisters.

	brothers	*sisters*
David's got …	....	....
His mother's got …	....	....
His father's got …	....	....
Ruiko's got …	....	....
Her mother's got …	....	....
Her father's got …	....	....

3 Have you got a big family?   `How many? Have you got …? writing; speaking`

Write numbers for your family or a family you know.

I've got .... brothers and .... sisters.

My mother's got .... sisters and .... brothers.

My father's got .... sisters and .... brothers.

Find out about families in your class.

Ask two people about their families, like this:

Have you got a big family?
How many brothers and sisters have you got?
How many brothers and sisters have your parents got?

Tell the class about the two people, like this:

Silvia's got a big family. She's got one brother and three sisters.
Her mother's got … and …, and her father's got … and ….

Mario hasn't got a big family. He's got no brothers or sisters.
His mother's got a sister and his father's got a brother.

HELP	In your language?
My friend's got …	....
twin brother/sister	....
an only child	....

✔ Quick Check

A Circle *yes* or *no*.

1. she's got = she is got   Y/N
2. I have got = I've got   Y/N
3. twenty-one = three × seven   Y/N
4. the son of your mother = your brother   Y/N
5. your father = the husband of your sister   Y/N

B Complete the answers.

1. Have you got any brothers? Yes, I ....
2. Has she got a sister? No, ... hasn't.
3. Have they got a father? Yes, ...
   ....
4. Has it got a window? No, it ....

C Write the family members under *Women* or *Men*.

sister   father   brother   wife   mother
husband   son   daughter

---

1 **In conversation – headaches and envelopes** ⎡ *some, any* ⎤

A 💿 Listen to Conversation 1 and underline *some* and *any*. Are they strong sounds?

Conversation 1

MAN: I've got a terrible headache, have you got any tablets?
WOMAN: I've got some in my bag ... Here you are.
MAN: Thanks.
WOMAN: Keep the bottle.
MAN: No, really, it's OK.
WOMAN: Go on, I've got some at home.
MAN: But I haven't got any money.
WOMAN: That's OK.

B Put *some* or *any* in the spaces in Conversation 2.

Conversation 2

A: Have you got .... envelopes?

B: There are .... in your room.

A: What about postcards?

B: Sorry, we haven't got .... postcards.

💿 Listen and check.

Write *some* or *any* in this rule.

> *Some/any* rule
>
> .... is for answers with *not*, and for questions.
>
> .... is for other answers.

Have you got words for *some* and *any* in your language?

Have Conversation 1 or 2 about:

− water

− vitamin C, B or E tablets

− magazines

− maps

2 In conversation with friends

A Read the conversations and match pictures A, B and C with the conversations.

1. A: I'm off to bed now. I'm really tired.
   B: OK. Goodnight, sleep well.
   A: Goodnight. See you in the morning.
   (Write your line) ....

A

B

2. A: See you later, then.
   B: What time?
   A: Oh, about seven.
   Write your line) ....
   ....

3. A: Are you happy here?
   B: Mmm, it's a really good flat.
   A: Is that one of your pictures?
   B: Mmm.
   A: The colours are lovely.
   (Write your line) ....

C

▭▭ Choose one of the conversations and listen to it. With a partner, write one final line of conversation, then practise the conversation.

B ▭▭ Listen to the final lines on the recording.

✔ Quick Check

A Write *some* or *any*.

1. Have you got .... tablets?

   No, sorry I haven't got ....

   Karin's got ....

2. I've got .... friends in Turkey.

3. Have they got .... pictures on the wall?

   Yes, they've got .... in the living room.

B Write different expressions after *See you*.

1. Bye. See you ....

2. Goodnight See you in the ....

C Write the words under the correct face.

happy   headache   tired   good
terrible   lovely

....

....

....

PERSONAL STUDY WORKBOOK

- *have got; some/any* practice
- reading and writing accommodation ads
- colour vocabulary
- visual dictionary – rooms and family
- reading – episode 5 of *Lost in time*

REVIEW OF UNIT 3

1 Find the letter in the numbers | numbers 30–100; listening |

📼 Listen and cross (✗) each number.

A	B
31 45 62 87 92	37 43 58 61
22 57 70 94 41	29 51 34 73
46 28 99 66 77	55 66 80 89
23 60 59 51 68	27 33 40 20
44 82 90 43 91	
20 97 76 33 40	

What letters have you got? Write the letters here.

A The letter is .... B The letter is ....

Choose a new letter. Say the numbers to a partner.

2 Is your ... nice? | pronunciation; speaking |

A 📼 Listen to these questions.

1. Is your office OK?
2. Is your car OK?
3. Is it old?

B 📼 Now listen again for the links.

1. Is your office OK?
2. Is your car OK?
3. Is it old?

Ask and answer the three questions in pairs.

C Ask and answer questions with one word from A and one from B, like this:

A: *Is your office new?*
B: *Yes, it is.*
A: *Is it nice?*
B: *Mm, it's OK.*

A | car   office   bedroom   flat |

B | old   new   big   small   nice   OK |

REVIEW OF UNIT 4

1 Are there any new things in our city? | vocabulary |

Are there any new things in your city? Find the English words for the new things. List the new words.

New things in our city

2 There's a new cinema | is/are there? speaking |

Talk about the new things, like this:

A: *There's a new **cinema** in Elm Street.*
B: *Is there?*
A: *Mm, it's really nice.*

A: *There are some new **shops** in Elm Street.*
B: *Are there?*
A: *Yeah, there's a new book shop and a nice coffee shop.*

DON'T FORGET YOUR SUNGLASSES

Language focus:	Vocabulary:
imperative forms	holidays and travel
prepositions (*to, for, in, on, under, by*)	countries and places
	days of the week

A HAVE A HOLIDAY

1 Holiday ads   vocabulary: nationalities

Look quickly at the ads for holidays and write the countries next to the nationalities.

BRAZIL
Holidays in Brazil
for less than you think!
**Call us now and get your
ticket to paradise**

Special Offer
A WEEK IN HUNGARY
*Includes air
travel, hotels* £220

SCANDITOURS
Travel to Norway and have
the holiday of a lifetime!
Departures
August 4, 11, 18, 25   £295
September 1, 18, 15   £240

BEAUTIFUL TURKEY
Seven nights from £350
Come to Turkey
this summer
GO travel

USA
Visit the USA this year.
✗ Coach tours around the States
✗ Visit fabulous San Francisco and
  see the beautiful scenery of
  Yosemite National Park.
✗ Take a helicopter flight over the
  Grand Canyon.
Call Windward Travel on 0171 360 1111

**Come to Greece,
home of the sun**
Return flights from London and Manchester
CALL NOW ON 0161 474 7555

EGYPT
Fly to Egypt this autumn and
visit the land of the pharaohs!
From £186 return

FRANCE
*Self-catering holidays in
the beautiful Loire Valley*
**Call us now on
0181 5437 6000.**

MEDICI TRAVEL
Holidays in Italy from £350
Call 0171 636 1551

Country	*Nationality*
....	Norwegian
....	American
....	Turkish
....	Brazilian
....	Greek
....	French
....	Hungarian
....	Italian
....	Egyptian

2 Radio ad `speaking; listening for imperative forms`

A  Listen to the ads and match *A* and *B*.

A	*B*
Come	at the Sheraton Hotel
Go	International Tours
Stay	a great time
Call	Qantas
Tell	to Italy
Have	your friends
Fly	to Greece

B Choose verbs from *A* to complete this ad.

 Listen and check.

TO ~~BRAZIL~~ FOR 10 DAYS FOR 2,000 DOLLARS.

.... Air New Zealand.

.... at the Excelsior Hotel in beautiful Bahia.

.... Cheap Travel on

303 67819 today!

3 Your holiday advert `adjectives; writing and speaking`

Put the words in the box into two lists.

beautiful	wonderful	awful	lovely	terrible	dirty

+ (nice)   − (not very nice)

....

....

....

Say the words in the lists in this sentence: *It's (wonderful)!*

Write a simple advert for a holiday in your country.
Write a nice advert or a not very nice advert.
Read your advert to a partner.

✔ Quick Check

A Tick the right picture.

1. Call Cheap Travel today.

2. Fly Air Lanka.

3. Tell your friends.

B Put in the missing word.

1. Stay the Sheraton hotel.
2. Come beautiful France.

3. Go New Zealand.
4. It wonderful!

5. Have great time.

1 Favourite cities   listening and discussion

Listen. Which two cities in the box are not in the conversation?

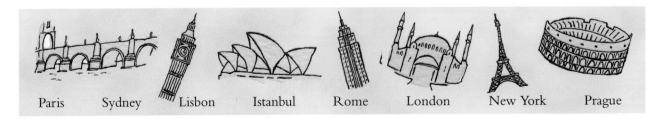

Paris   Sydney   Lisbon   Istanbul   Rome   London   New York   Prague

Write three of your favourite cities.

1 ....   2 ....   3 ....

Talk about your favourite cities with expressions from boxes A(djectives) and N(ouns).

A

| beautiful   busy   popular |
| modern   famous   interesting |
| old   fantastic   lovely   great |

N

| restaurants   buildings   beer |
| shops   parks   museums |
| universities |

Example: *My favourite city is Rome. It's a beautiful old city with lovely buildings and interesting museums. Copenhagen is also a favourite. It's got some interesting, modern buildings, great beer and some nice shops.*

2 Go to Oslo in November?   dual listening; *don't go*

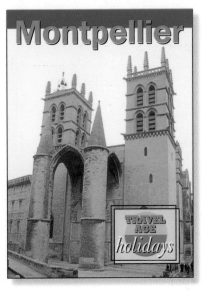

Where are the two cities on the brochures?

Listen to two people – one is a travel agent. Write the names of the four countries in their conversation.

| COUNTRIES: Brazil   Spain (Catalonia)   Slovakia   Greece   Turkey |
| France   Norway |

1. ....   2. ....   3. ....   4. ....

☐☐ Listen again. Is it a or b? Tick the correct boxes.

1. a. Have a look at this brochure of Athens. ☐
   b. Don't have a look at this brochure of Athens. ☐
2. a. Go to Oslo. ☐
   b. Don't go to Oslo. ☐
3. a. Don't take the brochure and read it at home. ☐
   b. Take the brochure and read it at home. ☐

3 Plan a tour | speaking: imperative forms; prepositions *to* and *for* |

Read the example. Write in three cities for a one-week tour. Add things to the *Don't forget* list.

☐☐ Listen to the example.

Example: A: *This is my tour. My guest is Mel Gibson. Day 1, fly to Dublin in Ireland and stay for two nights. Day 3, fly to Edinburgh in Scotland; stay for one night. Day 4, fly to Florence in Italy for three nights and fly home Day 7. What about you?*
B: *What about your 'Don't forget' list?*
A: *Oh, yes, don't forget your money and your camera … and your husband!*

Talk about your tour.

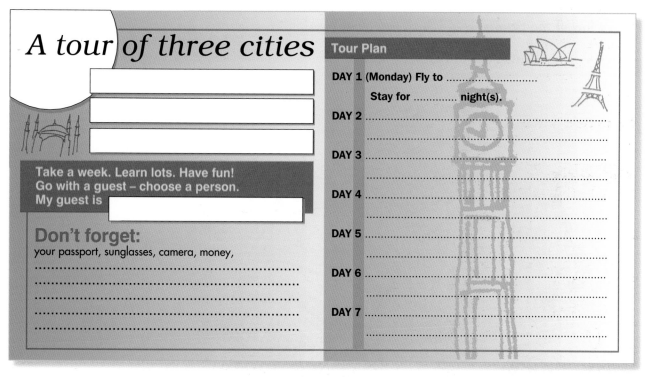

A tour of three cities

Tour Plan

DAY 1 (Monday) Fly to ....
        Stay for .... night(s).
DAY 2 ....
      ....
DAY 3 ....
      ....
DAY 4 ....
      ....
DAY 5 ....
      ....
DAY 6 ....
      ....
DAY 7 ....
      ....

Take a week. Learn lots. Have fun!
Go with a guest – choose a person.
My guest is [   ]

Don't forget:
your passport, sunglasses, camera, money,
....
....
....
....

✓ Quick Check

A Write *to* or *for* in the spaces.

1. Go .... London .... two nights.

2. Stay .... one night in Singapore.

3. Don't go .... London .... three nights.
   Go .... a week!

B Complete the nationalities.

Countries	Nationalities
Turkey	....
Ireland	....
USA	....
Greece	....
England	....

1 Today's Monday

vocabulary: days of the week

A Look at the days in this month. Say the days after Sunday.

Thursday   Saturday   Friday   Monday   Tuesday
Sunday   Wednesday

🎧 Listen and check.

B 🎧 Listen to the examples.

Examples:
1. A: *What day is it today?*
   B: *Thursday.*
2. A: *What day is it tomorrow?*
   B: *Friday.*
3. A: *What day is the 8th?*
   B: *Monday.*

Ask and answer two questions.

S	M	Tu	W	T	F	Sa
	1	2	3	4	5	6
7	8	9	10	11	12	13
14	15	16	17	18	19	20
21	22	23	24	25	26	27
28	29	30				

HELP	In your language?
weekend	....

2 Don't forget the tickets

vocabulary; writing notes

Match a picture with a day of the week in the note.

NOTE
Don't forget!
Monday   Get tickets for the holiday
Tuesday
Wednesday   Buy a film for the camera
Thursday
Friday   Go to the bank
Saturday   Phone Mum and Dad
Sunday   Restaurant 6 pm

A: ....

B: ....

C: ....

D: ....

E: ....

Read the note. Write a note for one or two days of *your* week.

Unit 6 DON'T FORGET YOUR SUNGLASSES

3 In hotel room number 512

prepositions of place; vocabulary: furniture

Look at these things.

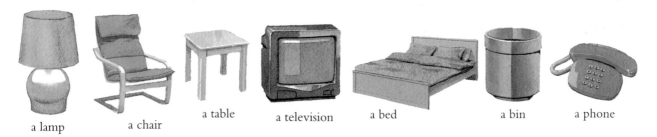

a lamp   a chair   a table   a television   a bed   a bin   a phone

Look at these pictures and answer the question *Where's the room key?*

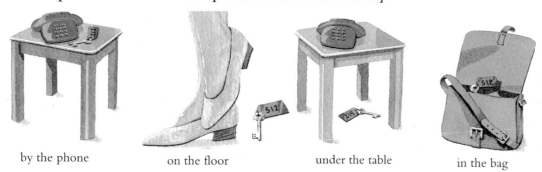

by the phone   on the floor   under the table   in the bag

Example: *Where's the room key?*
By the phone. (The key is by the phone.)

What's in the hotel room? Ask and answer the questions.

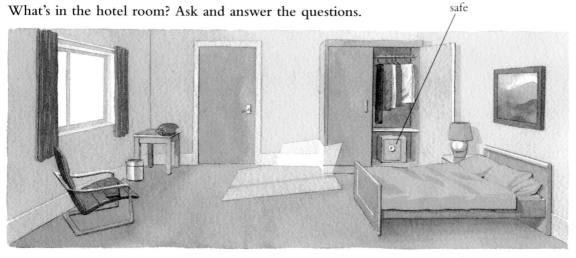

safe

Where's the phone?
.... the table, ... the door.

Where's the lamp?
.... the bed.

Where's the book?
.... the chair.

Where's the bin?
.... the window.

Where's the safe?
.... the wardrobe.

Listen to a conversation about room 512. Some things are different. What are two different things?

1. ....   2. ....

Where are these things in your bedroom? Ask and answer the questions.

1. Where's the bin?
2. Where's the lamp?
3. Where's the chair?
4. Where are your books?

HELP	In your language?
There aren't any books in my bedroom.	....
There isn't a bin.	....
bedside table	....

4 In conversation   conversation practice

📼 Listen and read.

ARNE: Come on Sunday, about nine. Is that OK?
ERICA: Yeah, that's fine.
ARNE: Don't forget your CDs.
ERICA: No, OK.
ARNE: See you on Sunday evening then.
ERICA: Yeah, see you. Bye.
ARNE: Bye.

1. Are there strong sounds on these words in the conversation?

Sunday	Y/N	on	Y/N
nine	Y/N	your	Y/N
CDs	Y/N	then	Y/N

2. Say *Yeah, that's fine* and *Yeah, see you. Bye* in your language.

Practise the same conversation in English. Change these things:

the day (not Sunday: *Thursday, Friday, Saturday*)
the time (not nine: *seven, eight, ten*)
the thing (not CDs: *photos, videos*)

✔ Quick Check

A Is it a or b? In spoken English, are strong sounds often on:

a. little words like *are, in, at* and *the*?
or
b. words for things, times, days and other information words?

B Write the words in these sentences in the right order.

1. bin under table is The the.
2. The by is door lamp the.
3. book your on Put table the.
4. bag my sunglasses in are Your.
5. put door Don't by bag your the.

C Answer the questions.

1. How many days are there in a week?

....

2. Which days start with T?

Thursday and ....

3. Which days start with S?

Saturday and ....

4. What are the three other days?

Monday, ... and ....

PERSONAL STUDY WORKBOOK

- vocabulary – adjectives; days of the week
- reading – travelling in London
- prepositions
- visual dictionary – hotel room and furniture and travel items
- reading – episode 6 of *Lost in time*

REVIEW OF UNIT 4

1 Auction | *How old ...?* numbers 100–1000; speaking; listening

Look at Number 1. Where is it from? How old is it?

Talk about Number 1 like this:

Number 1 is a beautiful/nice/lovely .... from ....
It's about .... years old.

📖 Listen and answer the questions.

1. Where is it from? ....
2. How old is it? ....
3. Who buys the chair?   a man? (Listen for *sir.*) ....
                   a woman? (Listen for *madam.*) ....
4. What is the final price? ....

In groups, auction numbers 2, 3 and 4.

2 Where are my keys? | *Where are ...?* (weak form); *perhaps; I think*; speaking

Make three cards like this.

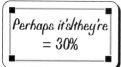

Perhaps it's/they're = 30%   *I think it's/they're =50%*   *It's/they're = 100%*

Now make cards like this.

📖 Listen and read. Ask and answer questions with a partner.

1. A: Where are my keys?
   B: Perhaps they're on the table.
   A: OK, thanks.

2. A: Where is my book?
   B: It's in my bag.
   A: Thanks.

3. A: Where are my tablets?
   B: I think they're on the bed.
   A: OK.

REVIEW OF UNIT 5

1 Survey | have got; vocabulary |

Write questions about people's homes.

Write three questions about rooms: kitchen, bathroom, living room, bedroom, toilet.

Write three questions about other things: telephone, radio, television, mobile phone, computer.

Examples: *Have you got a living room?*
How many bedrooms have you got?
Have you got a computer in your living room?

Ask two other learners these questions. Then ask about colours.

Example: What colour is your kitchen?

Write their answers like this:

Marcia has got two bedrooms, a green bedroom and a white bedroom.

2 Who's who? | vocabulary |

Look at this family. Fill the gaps in these sentences with family words from the box.

| father | mother | brother | sister | son | daughter | wife | husband |

1. Hi, my name's John. This is Jackie. She's my ....

2. I'm Helga. I've got two .... – Peter and Paul.

3. I'm Peter. I've got one ...., Paul, and three ....

4. We're Jackie and John. We've got three ....

5. I'm Paul. My .... is John and my .... is Jackie.

6. My name is Jackie. This is John. He's my ....

7. I'm John. Peter and Paul are my two ....

Write five sentences about a famous family in your country.

7

TIME FOR WORK

Language focus:
present simple: statements, questions, short answers
asking for and giving the time: *What's the time?/It's 6 o'clock.*
showing enthusiasm: *It's fantastic!*

Vocabulary:
jobs
workplaces

A WHAT'S THE TIME?

1 Clocks and watches | saying the time |

A Here are four pictures of clocks and watches. Match the pictures with the right sentences.

1. It's in London.

2. It's in her hand.

3. That's in your car.

4. It's in our office.

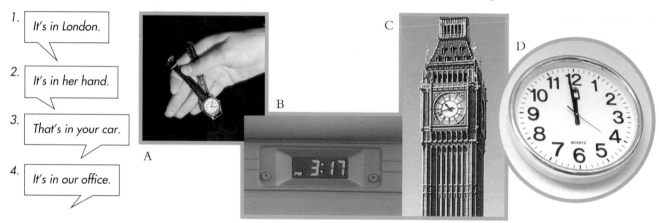

B 🔊 Look at the clocks, listen to the recording and repeat the times.

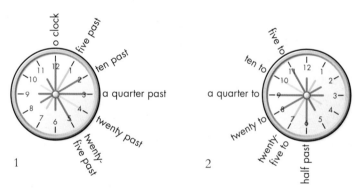

C 🔊 Listen and match the conversations with the clocks.

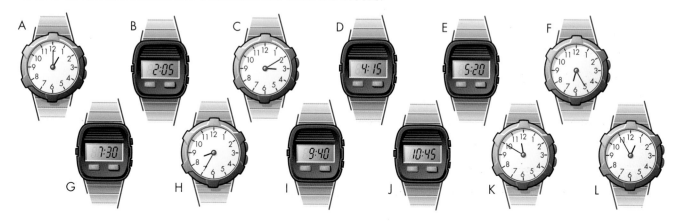

Lesson A WHAT'S THE TIME?   51

🎧 **Listen again and fill in the numbers you hear.**

1. Yes, it's half past ....
2. It's .... to one.
3. It's .... o'clock.
4. A quarter past ....!

5. Erm, yes, it's a quarter to ....
6. It's .... past five.
7. Yes, five past ....
8. It's .... to ten.

Ask and say the time in pairs, like this:

A: *What's the time?/What time is it?/Have you got the time?*
B: *It's ten past three.*
A: *Thanks a lot.*

2 Times of day | present simple; listening and speaking |

I get up early.

I get up late.

I have breakfast.

I go to work.

I get home.

🎧 **Listen to the conversation. Fill in the times you hear for the man and the woman.**

	man	*woman*	*you*	*friend*
1. get up	....	....	....	....
2. have breakfast	....	....	....	....
3. go to work	....	....	....	....
4. get home	....	....	....	....

Write your times under *you*. Then make conversations in pairs, like this:

A: *I get up at half past six.*
B: *That's very early!*
A: *What about you?*
B: *I get up at eight o'clock.*
A: *That's late.*

Write the other person's times under *friend*.

Talk to other learners about your times for:

– breakfast/lunch/dinner (with *have*)   – English classes/bed (with *go to*)

✔ Quick Check

A Write these times in words.
Example: *2.05*
five past two

1. 2.35 ....
2. 10.15 ....
3. 6.00 ....
4. 11.45 ....
5. 12.55 ....
6. 1.30 ....

B Write the numbers.
Example: *twenty to nine*
_8.40_

1. five to three ....
2. five past twelve ....
3. a quarter past eight ....
4. half past three ....
5. ten to four ....

C Write these sentences in the right order.

1. up eight at get o'clock I.
2. the What's time?
3. past It's six half.
4. five It's to a quarter.
5. you got Have the time?
6. seven have at breakfast I past a quarter.

1 What do you do?   [vocabulary]

⊂⊃ Here are some people at work. Listen to the recording, look at the pictures and find the job words in the list. Tick the job word.

> a shop assistant   an engineer   a waiter   a teacher   a businesswoman   a doctor

A: ....

B: ....

C: ....

E: ....

D: ....

F: ....

Match each person with one of these workplaces. Write the place next to the pictures.

> a hospital   an office   a laboratory   a department store   a restaurant   a school

2 Where do you work?   [present simple; listening]

⊂⊃ Listen to the interviews. Write a job word and a workplace word.

		job			*workplace*
1. I'm	a	**businesswoman**	I work in	an	**office**
2.	a/an	....		a/an	....
3.	a/an	....		a/an	....
4.	a/an	....		a/an	....
5.	a/an	....		a/an	....
6.	a/an	....		a/an	....

Here are some more jobs and workplaces. Is your job here? No? Look in a dictionary or ask your teacher.

photographer (studio)

lawyer (courtroom)

secretary (office)

scientist (laboratory)

nurse (hospital)

Now make conversations, like this:

A: *What do you do?*
B: *I'm a teacher.*
A: *Where do you work?*
B: *I work in a primary school.*

HELP	In your language?
I work for (Kodak).	....

3 When do you start and finish work? | present simple; speaking |

Listen and write the missing times. Write 24-hour clock times.

	1. teacher	2. waiter	3. shop assistant	4. businesswoman	5. engineer	6. doctor
Start	....	14.00	08.30	....	09.00	....
Finish	16.30	....	....	20.30	....	....

Ask five learners these questions and write their answers.

– When do you start work?   – When do you finish work?

✔ Quick Check

A Put the lines of this conversation in the right order.

A: you work Where do?
B: hospital I big work in a.
A: start you work When do?
B: morning the in o'clock eight At.
A: finish When you do?
B: in seven o'clock At the evening.

B Write one of these question words.

what   when   where

1. .... do you live?

2. ....'s your job?

3. .... do you finish work?

4. .... do you work?

C What are the missing words in this conversation? (There is ONE missing word in every line.)

A: What you do?
B: I'm engineer.
A: Where do work?
B: I usually work in laboratory.
A: What do you start?
B: About 9 o'clock in morning.
A: And do you finish?
B: I usually finish six o'clock at night.

1   She does but he doesn't! | present simple: questions and short answers |

Look at the pictures and listen to the conversations.

Listen again and repeat the conversations.

	Present simple	
Statements	**I/you/we/they work / don't work** in an office.	
	He/she works / doesn't work in a shop.	
Questions	**Do** you **work** in an office?	**Does she work** in a shop?
Answers	Yes, I **do**.	Yes, she **does**.
	No, I **don't**.	No, she **doesn't**.

Talk in threes. Ask and answer questions, like this:

A: *Do you work in an office?*
B: *No, I don't. I work in a shop.*
C: *Does B work in an office?*
A: *No, he/she doesn't. He/she works in a shop.*

2 What exactly do they do?

present simple: *he/she* form

Match the sentences with the pictures.

1. He **travels**.
2. She **writes**.
3. She **helps** people.
4. He **takes** money.
5. She **serves** customers.
6. He **buys**./She **sells**.
7. He **phones**.

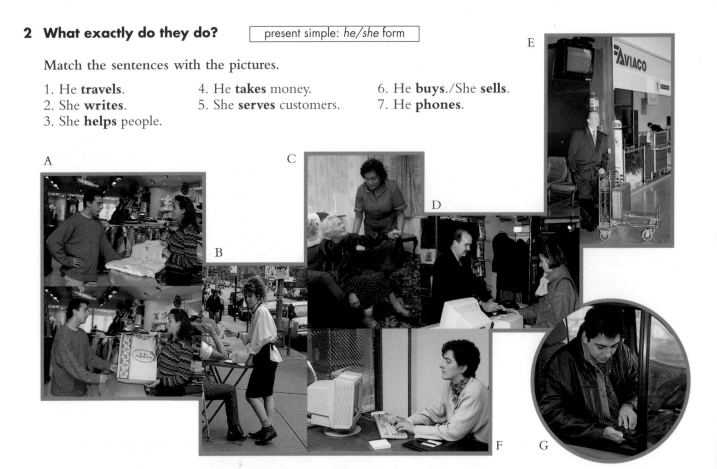

What do you think a waiter, a doctor, a shop assistant and a businesswoman do in their jobs?

Use these verbs: *buy, help, phone, sell, serve, take, travel, write.*

Talk to a partner and make lists, like this:

A waiter serves customers .....
        writes bills .....
        and takes money .....

📼 Listen to the four people talking and check your ideas. Tick your list.

Talk to your partner about the four jobs.

Example: A: *Does the waiter serve customers?*
            B: *Yes, he does. Does he write their bills?*
            A: *No, he doesn't. Does he take their money?*
            B: *Yes, he does.*

Now ask three other learners about their jobs. What exactly do they do?

3 Profiles

present simple; reading and writing

Read the text and answer these questions.

1. What is Katherine's job?
2. Where does she work?
3. What exactly does she do?

Write 30–40 words about one of the learners you talked to.

Katherine is a newspaper journalist. She works in New York. She writes about films and television. She takes her computer to the cinema. She watches films and writes about them. She often works in the evening and gets home late.

4 In conversation | showing enthusiasm |

A 📼 Listen to the recording and read the conversations.

1. A: What's your job?
   B: I'm a journalist.
   A: Do you like it?
   B: Yes, **it's great!**

2. A: What exactly do you do?
   B: I go to the cinema and write about films.
   A: Is it an interesting job?
   B: Yes – **it's fantastic!**

3. A: What time do you get up?
   B: Five o'clock in the morning.
   A: That's very early.
   B: **It's terrible!**

B 📼 Listen again. A is on the cassette. You say B's words.

In pairs, ask and answer questions. Use expressions from the conversations.

✔ Quick Check

A Fill the gaps with a job word and one of the verbs.

Jobs: businessman   doctor   shop assistant
teacher   waiter
Verbs: sell(s)   serve(s)   teach(es)   travel(s)
work(s)   write(s)

1. He's a ....
   He .... customers in a restaurant.

2. She's a ....
   She .... shoes and clothes to customers.

3. I'm a ....
   I .... in an office and I
   .... to lots of countries.

4. He's a ....
   He .... in a hospital and
   .... prescriptions.

5. She's a ....
   She .... children in a primary school.

B Fill in the gaps with one of these words:
do, does, don't, doesn't.

1. A: .... you work in a school?
   B: No, I ....

2. A: .... she travel to other countries?
   B: Yes, she ....

3. A: .... he serve customers?
   B: No, he ....

4. A: .... you like your job?
   B: Yes, I ....

PERSONAL STUDY WORKBOOK

- vocabulary of jobs and workplaces
- asking and saying what the time is
- listening to people talking about their work
- present simple verbs
- visual dictionary – jobs and time
- reading – episode 7 of *Lost in time*

REVIEW OF UNIT 5

1 Picture crossword | vocabulary |

Write the words in the crossword.

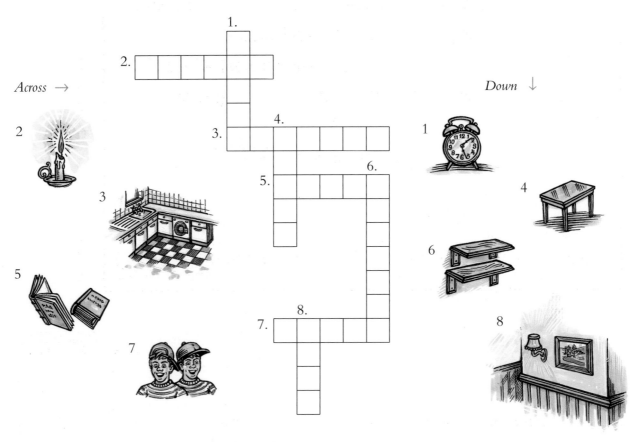

Across →

2

3

5

7

Down ↓

1

4

6

8

2 There's a pen under the ... | prepositions of place; writing |

There are four pens in this room. Find them. Write four sentences about the pens.

1. The first pen ....

2. The second pen ....

3. The ....

4. The ....

REVIEW OF UNIT 6

1 Come to our English class | imperatives; writing |

Complete the advert for your English class with words in the HELP box.

C........... to our English class in .... (your city).
L........... English with some lovely people.
E.......................... (number) **hours a week with a**
.... (adjective) **teacher from** .... (country).
D................ w............... . P.........................
.... (name of your school) **NOW!**

D............................... f...............................
English is the international language of travel!

HELP	In your language?
Don't forget	....
Don't wait	....
Enjoy	....
Phone	....
Learn	....
Come	....

Read your advert for a radio station.

2 At the travel agent's | prepositions |

Read this conversation and try to fill the gaps with the right words.

in	on	down	about	of	at

TRAVEL AGENT: Good morning. Come .... and sit ....

CUSTOMER: Thanks.

TRAVEL AGENT: Which country are you interested ....?

CUSTOMER: Greece. Do you have any information .... holidays .... Athens?

TRAVEL AGENT: Athens. Yes, I'm sure we have. Hang .... Yes, here you are.

CUSTOMER: Mm – lots .... old monuments – and the sea is quite near.

TRAVEL AGENT: How .... Italy? Florence is beautiful. Have a look .... the brochure.

CUSTOMER: What's it like .... this time .... the year?

TRAVEL AGENT: It's fantastic!

▭ Now listen to a recording of the conversation and check your answers.

Lesson D REVIEW AND DEVELOPMENT

INTERNATIONAL FOOD

Language focus:
expressing likes and dislikes: *like(s)/don't (doesn't) like*
asking about likes and expressing agreement:
Do you like ...? So do I. Me too.
conjunctions: *and* and *but*
question forms: *How long ...? How many ...?*
expressing lack of knowledge or information:
I don't know. I've no idea.
possessives: *'s*

Vocabulary:
food
months
language skills

A   I LIKE THAI FOOD ... SO DO I

1   Food from other countries   food vocabulary; nationalities

Name the restaurants for the meals A to G.

Example: *A is a meal from an Indian restaurant.*

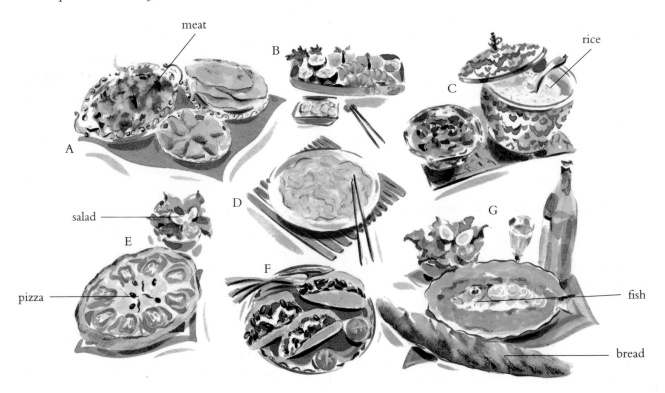

Look at the food words. Answer the questions.

1. What is white?
2. What is green?
3. What is cold?
4. What is hot?

HELP		In your language?
spicy		....
hot		....
cold		....

Have you got restaurants from these countries in your town?

2 I like Indian food ... so do I   expressing likes and agreeing

	She likes	I like
Indian food	☐	☐
Italian food	☐	☐
French food	☐	☐
Japanese food	☐	☐
American food	☐	☐
Chinese food	☐	☐
Thai food	☐	☐
Mexican food	☐	☐

I like Indian food.

So do I.

Me too.

▭ Listen and tick the food *she* likes.

Tick the food you like. Talk with other learners, like this:

A: *I like Italian food.*   B: *Me too.*   C: *So do I.*

3 Do you like ...?   questions with like; responses: *Yes, I do. No, I don't*; dual listening

▭ ▭ Listen to Version 1 or 2 of a conversation between Stefan and his teacher. Complete the sentences.

Version 1
Stefan likes ....

The teacher likes ....

Version 2
His sister likes ....

Her brother likes ....

In pairs ask and answer, like this:

A: *Do you like (Italian) food?*   B: *Yes, I do. / No, I don't.*
Tell the class your answers, like this:

A: *I like French food, Indian food and Thai food.*
   Antonio likes Mexican food, Japanese food and Italian food.

HELP	In your language?
I love Greek food.	....
I quite like Thai food.	....
I eat a lot of spicy food.	....

✔ Quick Check

A Find the endings for the beginnings and complete the word maths. Remember one country has no ending!

Example: *India + n = Indian + food = Indian food*

Beginnings	Endings		
Fr	ian		= ....
Ital	ese		= ....
Spa	k		= ....
Chin	ench		= ....
India	ese	+ food	= Indian food
Thai	nish		= ....
America	—		= ....
Japan	n		= ....
Gree	n		= ....

B Complete the table with *like* or *likes*.

I like French food.
He .... French food.
She .... French food.
Do you .... French food?

C Complete the sentences.

1. I like hamburgers but she li..... salad.
2. Miguel li..... rice and so .... I.
3. D.... you li..... Italian food?
   Yes, I ...., of course, and my wife li....
   Italian coffee.
   Mm so .... I. and I like Brazilian coffee.
   .... too.
4. Do you like Chinese food?
   No, I ....

D What is the general word for each group in 1 to 3.

1. Coca-Cola, coffee, beer. They are ....
2. hamburger, rice, salad, bread. They are ....
3. India, America, Japan. They are ....

1 Sandwich? No, thanks, John! | reading; vocabulary; *she/he likes/loves* |

Which title is for which text?

A sandwich? –
It's so simple

Sandwich? –
No, thanks, John

Sandwich? *– I'm in the international club*

Read one text. Tell a partner about it.

1. John is from Brisbane in Australia. He loves sandwiches! His sandwiches are interesting! He likes jam with cheese sandwiches, and meat sandwiches with fruit.

strawberry
banana } fruit
orange

jam
meat
cheese

2. Veronique is from France. In France people eat simple sandwiches. French bread with ham is a good example. A simple ham sandwich with a good, black coffee ... and no sugar... is wonderful.

3. Nobihiro is from Japan. He travels a lot to new countries. In international hotels he likes a good club sandwich. It's not Japanese, but chicken with bacon, fries and salad is nice and tasty.

bacon
fries

Ask and answer.

1. Does John like jam with cheese?
2. Does John like interesting sandwiches?
3. Does Veronique like coffee with sugar?
4. Does Nobihiro like sandwiches in Japan?

What about you? Do you like sandwiches?

HELP	In your language?
I don't know.	....
They're all right sometimes.	....

2 I don't like coffee with sugar
listening; don't/doesn't like; and/but

📖 Listen and complete.

Do you like coffee?

Good coffee, yes, but I don't like ....
with ....
My husband doesn't like ....
but he loves ....

Do you like sandwiches?

I like simple .... but my wife ....
sandwiches with different things in. But we ....
like the sandwiches in some of the coffee shops.

Talk about:

– food/drink you don't like (*I don't like …*)
– food/drink a friend, husband or wife doesn't like (*My friend doesn't like …*)

3 In our family we like ...
writing with I/we like

This is part of a letter from you to a friend in England. Complete the sentences about food and (1) your friend, (2) your family, (3) people in your country. Use a dictionary.

My friend, _____ , likes_____
with _____ but I don't like _____ .
My (mother) doesn't like _____ .
    In our family we don't like _____ but
we eat a lot of _____ . People in our country
love _____ .
    See you in July,

✓ Quick Check

A Write in the five apostrophes ('). Complete the long form of the verbs.

1. I dont like coffee. = I do .... like coffee.
2. She doesnt like meat. = She ...... not like meat.
3. Thats terrible. = That .... terrible.
4. Theyve got some sandwiches = They .... some sandwiches.
5. They dont like the bread. = They .... not like the bread.

B Write *and* or *but*.

1. I like meat .... I don't eat fish.
2. He likes coffee .... cheese.
3. We love bread .... we love rice.
4. They like bread .... not sandwiches.
5. I don't like wine .... I don't like tea.

Write Sentence B3 in your language.

C Give an example of:

1. a fruit ....
2. meat ....
3. a drink ....
4. a meal ....

1 In conversation | possessive 's; *I don't know/I've no idea* |

Study this sentence:

My tea, your tea, Miguel's tea and my mother's tea are in the kitchen.

Complete these sentences.

1. Miguel**'s** tea means the tea of ....
2. My mother**'s** tea means the tea of ....

📼 **Listen and read this conversation.**

VACLAV: When's Jana's dinner party?
HELEN: Er, sorry, I've no idea.
VACLAV: Is it on Saturday, do you think?
HELEN: I don't know. Ask Tomo, he's Jana's friend.
VACLAV: OK, thanks, bye.
HELEN: Bye.

Tick the correct box or answer the question.

1. Vaclav and Helen are probably friends.   Yes ☐   No ☐
2. What's the name of Jana's friend? ....
3. Is Jana's party on Saturday?   Yes ☐   No ☐   I'm not sure ☐
4. I've no idea = I don't know.   Yes ☐   No ☐

Practise the conversation with different names.

2 Phone language | listening for sounds; phone vocabulary |

A 📼 **Listen and say these names.**

– Smith's restaurant – Schmidt's restaurant – Smee's restaurant

B 📼 **Listen. What is the name of the restaurant in this phone conversation?**

WOMAN: Is that (*name*)?
MAN: Sorry? What? It's a bad line.
WOMAN: Is that (*name*)?
MAN: I'm sorry ... is that who?
WOMAN: (*name*).
MAN: What number do you want?
WOMAN: 288 40212.
MAN: You've got the wrong number;
             this is 288 40202.
WOMAN: Oh, I'm sorry.
MAN: That's OK, bye.

C 📼 **Listen to the conversation on a good line. Check your answer.**

Practise the conversation.

3 Two hours a week for three months

listening; reading; months; *How long ...? How many ...?*

a month   a week

A 🔊 Listen and tick the months. Two are in the wrong order. Which two?

What is the sixth month? How many days has it got?

B 🔊 Listen and complete the information for Ludmila.

Write the information for your course.

Ludmila's English Course

How long is your English course?   *3 months – July.*
.... How many weeks? .... weeks
How many hours a week? .... hours per week
What are the days and times a week? Tuesday and
.... from .... till .... *9* p..........
What week of your course is this week? ....

My English Course

How long is your English course? ....
How many weeks? .... weeks
How many hours a week? .... hours per week
What are the days and times a week? ....
.... from .... till ....
What week of your course is this week? ....

Tick the boxes for you.

My Progress in English

	Good progress	OK	Slow progress
Listening	☐	☐	☐
Speaking	☐	☐	☐
Reading	☐	☐	☐
Writing	☐	☐	☐
Vocabulary	☐	☐	☐
Grammar	☐	☐	☐
Pronunciation	☐	☐	☐
English homework	☐	☐	☐

✔ Quick Check

A Answer the questions.

1. Put the months in order from 1–12. Start with January.
2. How many days are there in one week?
3. How many days are there in June?
4. How many days are there in March?
5. What is the second month?
6. What is the fifth month?
7. Is August a summer month in Australia?
8. There are 24 hours in one ....
9. When is your birthday?
10. When is your teacher's birthday?

B Rewrite these with 's.

1. The birthday of my sister
   = My ....
2. The birthday of Karel
   = ...

3. The birthday of his father
   = His ....
4. The birthday of John's grandmother
   = John's ....

C Put the words in the right order in some of the lines (★) of the conversation.

★A: Hi, there John is?
★B: Sorry, want to to you who speak do?
 A: John.
★B: who John?
 A: John Smith.
★B: number got you've wrong the Sorry.
★A: sorry, I'm bye.
 B: Bye.

▭ Listen and check.

PERSONAL STUDY WORKBOOK

- reading an airline menu
- *to like* practice
- *and/but* in a letter

- visual dictionary – food
- reading – episode 8 of *Lost in time*

D REVIEW AND DEVELOPMENT

REVIEW OF UNIT 6

Please come | vocabulary: days of the week; speaking |

Complete the conversation. Use the sentences in the Sorry box and write some others.

A: Come on Monday.
B: Sorry, I've got an English class on Monday.
A: How about Tuesday?
B: Sorry, I've got a meeting.
A: OK. How about Wednesday?
B: Sorry, ...
A: Mmm. How about Thursday?
B: Sorry, ...
A: OK How about Friday?
B: I'm sorry I'm ...
A: How about Saturday?
B: Sorry, I'm ...
A: How about Sunday?
B: Mmm. Yes, that's fine.
A: Is it? Are you sure?
B: Mmm.
A: Great!!!!
B: Oh! Sorry, I've got a ...

SORRY BOX

Sorry, I've got an English class on Monday.

I've got a conference.

I'm at the library.

I'm in Scotland.

I'm at work.

....

....

(Write one or two.)

Say the conversation with a partner. Record your conversation and listen to it.

REVIEW OF UNIT 7

Times of the day | present simple; writing and speaking |

Write about a friend or someone in your family – your partner, children, brother or sister. What does he or she do in the day? When does he or she do these things? Follow the example.

Name: *Paulo*		Name	
Time	What does he/she do?	Time	What does he/she do?
6.45	*He has breakfast.*	....	....
7.15	*He goes to work.*	....	....
		....	....
		....	....
		....	....
		....	....
		....	....

Now talk to your partner, like this:

A: *Who is the person?*
B: *My sister.*
A: *What's her name?*
B: *Isabelle.*
A: *Tell me about Isabelle.*
B: *She has breakfast at 7 o'clock and she leaves home at a quarter past eight.*

9

MONEY! MONEY! MONEY!

Language focus:
talking about prices: *How much ...?*
asking for things in shops: *I'd like ...*
asking someone to repeat something: *Pardon? Sorry?*

Vocabulary:
presents
money and currencies
electrical goods

A SHOPPING

1 Shops   vocabulary

You are at the airport. Where can you buy these things? Find the right shop, A, B, C, D, E or F.

earrings ....   camera ....   CDs ....   personal stereo ....

television ....   T-shirt ....   jeans ....   necklace ....

shoes ....   newspapers ....   postcards ....   things for children ....

A    B    C    D    E    F

What other things are in these shops? Write lists.

2 At the airport   listening; vocabulary

A ⬭ Listen to some people at an airport. They are on their way home. Which shops are they in? Fill in the spaces.

Which shop? (A–F)	What do they buy?
1.	....
2.	....
3.	....
4.	....
5.	....

B 🎧 Listen again. What do the people buy? Choose from the list and fill the spaces.

a small camera   cassettes   CDs   a pair of earrings   a magazine   a necklace
a pair of shoes   a T-shirt   a teddy bear   a television

C 🎧 Who do they buy things for? Listen and choose a person for each conversation.

partner (= husband or wife/boyfriend or girlfriend)   brother   sister   son
daughter   grandson   granddaughter   friend

1. ....   3. ....   5. ....

2. ....   4. ....

3 Presents | I'd like...; speaking |

You want to buy some presents for your family and friends.
Choose things from the shops. Write a list, like this:

Work in pairs. Make conversations, like this:

ASSISTANT: *Can I help you?*
CUSTOMER: *Yes, I'd like some earrings, please.*
ASSISTANT: *Are they a present for someone?*
CUSTOMER: *Yes, they are. They're for my mother.*

4 Questions | speaking; writing |

Answer these questions.

1. Have you got an umbrella?
2. What colour is it?
3. Have you got a TV?
4. Is it big or small?
5. Would you like a new T-shirt?
6. What colour would you like?

Now ask another learner the questions and write his or her answers.

Presents to buy

mother: earrings

partner: watch

son or daughter: CD

brother or sister:
red T-shirt

friend: cassette

✓ Quick Check

A Write the words in the correct order.

1. CUSTOMER: have this please can I necklace?
   ASSISTANT: course yes of present it a is?
2. CUSTOMER: T-shirt got a have you green?
   ASSISTANT: have we yes or small large.
3. ASSISTANT: you help can I?
   CUSTOMER: please that camera Japanese small
   like I'd.
4 CUSTOMER: umbrella I'd please an like.
   ASSISTANT: a for a man woman is it or?

B What are the long forms?

1. It's for my daughter.
2. I'd like a small television.
3. We've got black, white or red.
4. It's for my son. He's only five weeks old.
5. They're for my mother.

C What can you listen to, what can you read,
what can you see? Match the verbs with the
nouns.

Verbs: listen to   read   watch
Nouns: book   cassette   CD   film   football match
magazine   newspaper   personal stereo   television

B MONEY MATTERS

1 Prices   vocabulary; listening

Where is the money from?
Match the countries and the currencies.

Australia	lira
Britain	drachma
Germany	yen
Greece	dollar
Italy	pound
Japan	dollar
Spain	deutschmark
United States	peseta

Listen and write the prices.

1. .... yen   3. .... pounds   5. .... pesetas   7. .... dollars

2. .... lire   4. .... drachma   6. .... deutschmarks   8. .... dollars

2 Souvenirs   prices; listening

A Four people talk about their holiday souvenirs. Listen for the name of the country and the souvenirs. Fill in the spaces.

	Example	1.	2.	3.	4.
Country	Japan	....	....	....	....
Souvenir	camera	....	....	....	....

B Listen to the conversations and write the prices of the souvenirs in the price tags.

HELP	In your language?
How much is it?	....
How much are they?	....

70

3 Prices

How much are these things? Write a list of prices in your money and in pounds or dollars. Don't show other people.

Make conversations in pairs, like this:

A: *Hello. Can I help you?*
B: *Yes, how much is this necklace?*
A: *It's a hundred pounds.*
B: *That's very expensive!*

✔ Quick Check

A Correct the mistakes.

1. Spain are a very nice country.
2. That really expensive.
3. This teddy bear is two hundreds pounds.
4. My shoes is from London.
5. We really like moderns paintings.
6. How much are this necklace?

B Fill the gaps in these sentences with one of these words: *for, from, in, on, to.*

1. My T-shirt's got my name .... it.

2. I've bought a present .... my best friend.

3. My shoes are .... Italy.

4. Have a nice holiday .... France.

5. Welcome .... New York.

C Find the right answers to the questions.

1. How much is that T-shirt?
2. Have you got any postcards?
3. How much are these shoes?
4. Who are the sunglasses for?
5. Where are you from?
6. Who's the necklace for?

a. No, we haven't.
b. I'm from Scotland.
c. They're for my little sister.
d. It's twenty pounds.
e. It's for my mother.
f. They're £100. `

1 Things in a catalogue   reading; vocabulary

Read these descriptions of things in a catalogue. Match them with the photographs.

WALLET
Black or brown.
Real leather.
For notes and credit cards.

CODE: MLW66

MICRO RECORDER
Two-speed micro-cassette recorder.
Two hours of recording time. Speak
and the recorder starts.

CODE: MCR22

NIGHT WATCH
Quartz watch. White face and
large black numbers. Silver
hour and minute hands and
red second hand.

CODE: WWN 2

DESK FAX
Answer machine and fax in one.
Black or green.

CODE: DFX–33

2 On the phone   listening

Listen to the telephone conversation and complete this form.

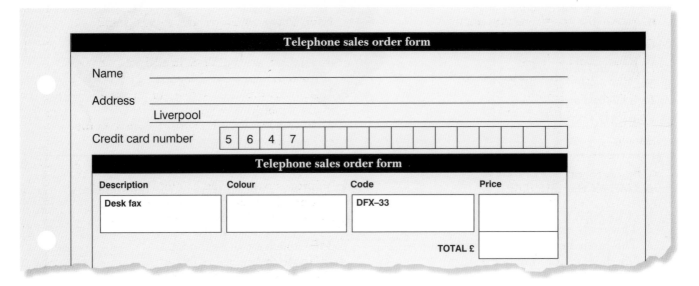

Telephone sales order form			
Name			
Address			
Liverpool			
Credit card number 5 6 4 7			

Telephone sales order form			
Description	**Colour**	**Code**	**Price**
Desk fax		DFX–33	
		TOTAL £	

3 Role play   speaking

In pairs, take turns to be the customer and the assistant. Use some of these questions.

Customer: *Have you got a …?*   *Can I have …?*   *How much is …?*
Assistant: *What colour …?*   *What's your name/address/card number?*

Partner A (Customer):   Find the price of the watch, then order it.
Partner B (Sales assistant): Tell the customer the price of the watch (you decide), then ask for
his or her name and address.

Partner A (Customer):   Find the price of the wallet, then order it. (You want a brown wallet.)
Partner B (Sales assistant): Tell the customer the price of the wallet (you decide), find out the
colour he or she wants, then ask for his or her name and address.

4 In conversation | asking someone to repeat something |

📼 Listen and read.

POLLY: Look at this micro recorder.
It's a very small cassette recorder.
MARIA: What did you say?
POLLY: This is a very small cassette recorder.
You speak and the recorder starts.
MARIA: Pardon?
POLLY: You speak and it starts.
MARIA: Is it expensive?
POLLY: About £300, I think.
MARIA: Sorry?
POLLY: About £300.

Work in pairs. Have conversations like this about the digital diary and the mini-fridge.

DIGITAL DIARY
Small screen with clock and alarm. Keep your addresses and telephone numbers in one place. 500 names and numbers.
£30

CODE: DD1X

MINI-FRIDGE
For offices or small shops. Keep snacks and drinks cold. 486 mm x 502 x 564
£200

CODE: MFW–101

✔ Quick Check

A Match the questions and answers.

Questions
1. What would you like?
2. What's the code number?
3. What colour do you want?
4. How do you want to pay?
5. What's your card number?

Answers
a. By credit card.
b. Black, please.
c. 3247 9572 6129 3726.
d. I'd like a mini-TV, please.
e. It's MTV32.

B Look at the catalogue descriptions and answer these questions.

1. What has a face and three hands?
2. What is the opposite of *large*?
3. How many minutes are there in one hour? Write a word.
4. How many words for colours are there in the six descriptions?
5. Find two words for very *small*.

C Write a catalogue description of one of your things, for example a watch, a pen, glasses, a radio. Write like this:

WALLET
– Black or brown.
– Real leather (not plastic).
– For notes and credit cards.
CODE: MLW66

PERSONAL STUDY WORKBOOK

- vocabulary of money, prices and shopping
- listening to people buying things
- reading descriptions in a catalogue
- ordering things by telephone: listening and speaking activities
- visual dictionary – a student's room
- reading – episode 9 of *Lost in time*

REVIEW OF UNIT 7

1 Departure times | times; speaking |

Fill the spaces with one of these times. Don't show other people.

| 06.30 | 07.05 | 09.15 | 10.50 | 11.45 | 13.50 | 14.25 | 16.20 | 18.00 |
| 20.05 | 22.10 | 23.30 |

International departures

Destination	Flight	Time	Gate
Madrid	IB632	....	16
Perth	QF235	....	10
Istanbul	BA39	....	17
Bangkok	MAS724	....	22
Berlin	LH212	....	12
Tokyo	JAL831	....	18

Have conversations with another learner, like this:

A: *What time is the flight to Madrid?*
B: *It's half past six in the morning.*

2 Verb endings | pronunciation |

CD Listen. What are the sounds at the end of these verbs, /s/, /z/ or /ɪz/?

1. **works**   He works in a café.
2. **teaches**   She teaches in a primary school.
3. **goes**   He goes to school at 8 o'clock.
4. **finishes**   She finishes work at 6 o'clock.
5. **helps**   He helps his brother.
6. **watches**   She watches television in the evening.
7. **phones**   He phones his sister every day.
8. **writes**   She writes postcards to her family.

CD Listen again and check.

REVIEW OF UNIT 8

1 Do you like international fast food? vocabulary; speaking

What international fast food restaurants are there near your home or in your part of the city? Write a list of the names and the type of food.

Do you like these restaurants? Tell a partner about the good and bad restaurants.

Examples: *I like … a lot.*
I don't know that restaurant.
The service is quick/good/awful.
The food is cheap/expensive/fresh.
My son/daughter likes … but I …

2 Seasonal geography months and seasons; speaking

Write the names of the months for the seasons in these cities.

Winter in Buenos Aires ....
Summer in Oslo ....
Spring in Melbourne ....
Autumn in Edinburgh ....

Ask a partner questions about other cities.

Example: *What are the (spring) months in (Paris)?*

10

CLOTHES FOR WORK AND PLAY

Language focus:
questions: *whose?/which?*
possessive *'s*
too + adjective
compliments: *I like your ... It suits you.*

Vocabulary:
clothes
jobs

A WORK AND CLOTHES

1 What do people wear for work? | present simple; frequency adverbs; reading |

Match the four people with their words.

I often wear a skirt, a pullover and flat shoes.

I always wear a suit, a white shirt and a tie.

I usually wear jeans, a shirt and a jacket. I never wear a tie.

I always wear a suit, a white blouse and high-heeled shoes.

1. Pierre, 22, is a photographer.

2. Monica, 39, is a university teacher.

3. Angela, 24, works for an international company.

4. Mark, 42, is director of a German computer business.

2 At the weekend | present simple; listening |

Pierre, Monica, Angela and Mark don't work at the weekend. What do you think they wear? Talk to another learner and then write lists.

pullover

sweatshirt

blouse

T-shirt

shoes

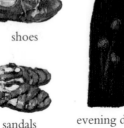
evening dress

skirt

trousers

jeans

cap

shorts

sandals

Unit 10 CLOTHES FOR WORK AND PLAY

📖 Listen to the four people talking. Check your guesses.

📖 Listen again and fill the spaces with a clothes word.

1. MARK: I usually wear trousers – not .... – and a shirt. I sometimes

    wear a ....

    INTERVIEWER: Do you wear a ....?

2. MONICA: I usually wear just jeans and a .... And .... – I

    love my ....

3. ANGELA: And at discos, I usually wear a .... and a bright blouse.

4. PIERRE: Shorts and a .... On the beach I sometimes wear a baseball

    cap and ....

Ask another person questions about the four people, like this:

A: *What does Monica wear at the weekend?*   B: *She wears sandals.*
or
A: *Who wears sandals at the weekend?*   B: *Monica does.*

3 Survey   speaking

Ask other learners *What do you wear at the weekend?*

Write their answers in the table. Look at the example.

Name	What do you wear at weekends?	What do you do?
Laura	jeans, T-shirt, sandals	cinema/parties
1.		
2.		
3.		

Ask *What do you do at the weekend?* Use words from the lists. Write the answers in the spaces.

play	go to	watch	work
sports (football/ tennis/golf) games	the shops the beach the swimming pool the cinema parties concerts	TV sport	at home in the garden

✔ Quick Check

A Here are some answers. What are the questions?

1. I usually wear a suit and tie for work.
2. No, I wear flat shoes at the weekend.
3. No, it's not my cap.
4. No, my pullover's black.
5. I always wear jeans and a T-shirt at the weekend.

B Who usually wears these clothes – men, women or men and women? Make three lists.

blouse   cap   dress   high-heeled shoes   jacket   jeans   pullover   sandals   shirt   shorts   skirt   suit   sweatshirt   T-shirt   tie   trainers

C What do you wear for work? Write lists of the clothes you wear:

– in the summer;
– in the winter.

1 Uniforms | whose?, which? |

Look at these photos of people in uniforms. Match the photos with the words for their jobs.

| fire fighter | baseball player | nun | soldier | racing driver | nurse | school student |

Brendan

Michael

Tom

Maria

Jenny

Dave

Jerry

Now look at these small pictures.

Talk in pairs. Ask questions, like this:

A: *Whose dress is this?*   B: *It's Jenny's dress./It's the nurse's dress.*
or
A: *Which dress is Jenny's/the nurse's?*   B: *This dress (is Jenny's).*

Possessions
Question: **Whose** cap is this?   Question: **Which** cap is **Jerry's**?
Answer: It's **Jerry's** cap.   Answer: This cap is **Jerry's**.
          It's **Jerry's**.
Notice the 's in Jerry's.

2 Discussion   speaking

Talk in twos or threes.

– Do you wear a uniform in your job?   – Do you like uniforms?   – Which uniform would you like to wear?

3 Famous faces   *whose?, which?; speaking*

Here are six famous mouths. Whose mouths are they? Ask each other questions.
Can you agree?

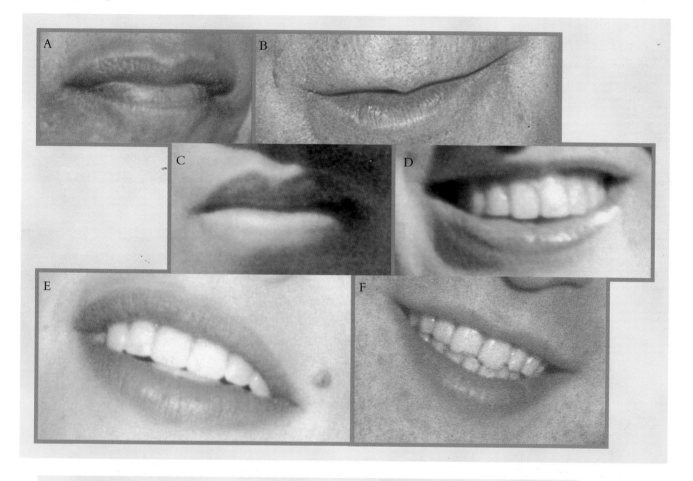

Brad Pitt   Margaret Thatcher   Tiger Woods   John Lennon   Martina Hingis
Catherine Deneuve   Nelson Mandela   Cindy Crawford   Pope John Paul II

🎧 Listen and check your answers. Have you got the same answers as other people in
the class? Check, like this:

A: *Which mouth is Cindy Crawford's?*   B: *This mouth is (Cindy Crawford's).*

4 Your possessions   vocabulary; speaking

Work with three or four other people. Close your eyes, then put something of yours
on the table. Guess who the things belong to.

Example: A: *Whose bag is this?*
          B: *I think it's Paul's.*
          C: *I think it's Maria's.*
          A: *Maria, is it your bag?*
          D: *No, it isn't.*
          B: *Is it your bag, Paul?*
          E: *Yes, it is.*

A Which question words are missing?

what   which   who   whose

1. A: ....'s that?

   B: It's my father.

2. A: .... pullover is this?

   B: It's Tony's.

3. A: .... does a policeman wear on his head?

   B: A helmet.

4. A: .... dress is Sarah's?

   B: The red dress.

5. A: .... jacket is this?

   B: It's my jacket.

6. A: .... shoes do you wear at the weekend?

   B: I usually wear sandals.

B *'s* or *s*? Choose the right word.

1. Nurse's/Nurses wear uniform's/uniforms.
2. This is my father's/fathers jacket.
3. Are you Paul's/Pauls brother?
4. Do racing driver's/drivers always wear helmet's/helmets?
5. These boot's/boots are my brother's/brothers.

C Which word is different? What are the other two words?

Example: helmet, cap, shoe
Shoe is different. The other two words are hats.

1. nurse, soldier, doctor
2. student, baseball player, footballer
3. trousers, pullover, shorts
4. boots, sandals, jacket
5. dress, shirt, tie

C   IT'S LOVELY

1 Conversations | *too;* listening |

🎧 Listen to four conversations. Who are the people?

Match a person from List A with a person from List B.

A	*B*
boy	daughter
shop assistant	manager
waiter	customer
mother	boyfriend
girl	father

It's **too** expensive.

🎧 Listen to Conversations 2, 3 and 4 again and find the right picture: A, B or C.

Conversation 2

A   B   C

Conversation 4

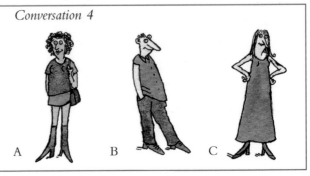

A   B   C

Conversation 3

A   B   C

2 In conversation   compliments; listening and speaking

A  Listen and read this conversation.

A: Hi! How are you?
B: Fine. I like your hair!
A: Do you really?
B: Yes, it's great!
A: What about the colour?
B: It really suits you.
A: Do you think it's too short?
B: No, it looks lovely.

B Listen again. A is on the cassette.
You are B. Say B's words.

Make similar conversations with other learners. Talk about hair, clothes, jewellery, shoes or other things. Use some of these words:

red	blue	yellow	big	small	long	short	bright

3 A letter from Florida   reading and writing

Here is part of a letter from a friend. Fill the gaps with one of these words.

about	beach	big	nightclub	hot	like	loud	photo	wear

I'm on holiday in Florida. I love America, but
there are problems. There is a
.... near the hotel — the music
is too .... And I don't like the
weather. It's too .... for me.
Here's a .... of me in my holiday
clothes. Do you .... my T-shirt?
And what .... my hat? Do you
think it's too .... for me? I think
it's fantastic! Don't worry, I only
.... it on the ....

See you next week.

Love,
Paula

It's too loud!

 Compare answers with another person, then listen and check.

Write a letter like this to a friend.

A Fill the gaps in these sentences with *to* or *too*.

1. She wants .... go .... Turkey.
2. This jacket is .... expensive.
3. I usually go .... the beach on Sunday mornings.
4. A: The plane leaves at ten o'clock.
   B: That's .... late for me.
5. That cap belongs .... me.

B All the lines have *one* word missing. What is the word and where does it go?

1. A: You like my new shoes?
   B: Yes, do.
2. A: What do you think the colour?
   B: I like it. Red suits.

3. I'd like buy these shoes, please.
4. This T-shirt is too small me.
5. I like your jeans – look fantastic!

C Somebody says these things to you. Are they good or bad? Put ✔ or ✗.

1. Your shoes are too big for you. ....

2. Your hair looks lovely. ....

3. I really like your earrings. ....

4. White jeans don't really suit you. ....

5. Your jacket's too small. ....

6. That uniform suits you. ....

PERSONAL STUDY WORKBOOK

- vocabulary of clothes and uniforms
- saying nice things to other people: listening and speaking activities
- pronunciation work
- visual dictionary – clothes
- reading – episode 10 of *Lost in time*

D **REVIEW AND DEVELOPMENT**

REVIEW OF UNIT 8

1 I eat a lot of pasta | present simple; vocabulary; speaking |

Look at this 'pizza' diagram for the things this man eats.

Draw a pizza for you. Write the names of the foods.

Talk to a partner about the things you eat.

Example: *I eat a lot of (vegetables).*
I don't eat a lot of (meat).

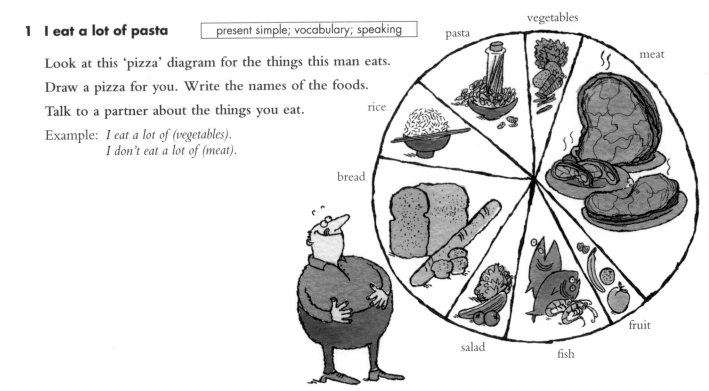

vegetables

pasta

meat

rice

bread

fruit

salad

fish

2 Eight glasses of water How many? reading and speaking

Read this. How many different drinks are there?

Some people say, 'Drink eight glasses of water a day; it's good for you'. Some people like wine, coffee, beer, fruit drinks and tea and they don't drink a lot of water.

📖 Listen and repeat the parts of question 1.

1. How many glasses of water do you drink a day?
2. How many cups of coffee do you drink a day?
3. How many cups of tea do you drink a day?
4. How many glasses of wine do you drink a day?
5. How many glasses/cups of .... (write a drink here) do you drink a day?

Ask two learners these questions. Talk about the answers you've got.

REVIEW OF UNIT 9

1 Prices How much? speaking; vocabulary

Match these words with the pictures.

camera   CD   necklace   shoes   sunglasses   T-shirt   wallet

How much do these things cost? Decide the price in dollars ($), pounds (£) or your currency. Don't show other people your prices.

In pairs make shop conversations, like this:

A: *Can I help you?*
B: *Yes. How much is the red T-shirt?*
A: *It's twenty-five dollars.*
B: *That's cheap/expensive!*

2 Money and countries vocabulary

Find the currencies and the right countries.

Example: undop = *pound*   *Britain*

1. tesepa   = ...
2. rolald   = ...
3. eyn   = ...
4. madarch   = ...
5. skuthracmed = ...

Lesson D REVIEW AND DEVELOPMENT   83

11

ARE YOU THE RIGHT PERSON FOR YOUR JOB?

Language focus:
can, can't for ability
question forms: *Why (not)?*
because
What about ...?
use of impersonal pronoun *you*
apologies and excuses

Vocabulary:
applying for jobs
work skills

A   YOU'VE GOT THE JOB!

1   I'm a TEN!   vocabulary; *can* for ability; *Why? Because ...*

Give a score (between 1 and 10) for you for sentences 1–5.

1. I can write good business letters.   (..../10)

2. I can write good business reports.   (..../10)

3. I like people.   (..../10)

4. I can talk to people on the phone.   (..../10)

5. I can use computers.   (..../10)

Talk about your good scores, 6–10, like this:

A: *I think I'm a 6 for number 1.*
B: *Why?*
A: *Because I can write good letters. What about you?*

2   Yes, I can   dual listening; *can* questions; short responses

CD   CD   Listen to a woman answering questions from Exercise 1. Tick (✓) the things she can do. Cross (✗) the things she can't do.

business letters   ☐   people   ☐   computers   ☐
reports   ☐   phone   ☐

Complete two of the *Can ...?* questions from the recording.

1. Can you ....?

2. Can you ....?

What is the answer to your two questions? Is it *Yes, I can* or *No, I can't*? Listen a second time and check.

3 Here's my report   writing sentences with *can*

Ask the same *can* questions and write a report for two people in your class.

Read your reports to the two people.

What about your teacher? Can she/he do some of these things?

> Quick report on ....
> .... *can/can't* write good
> business letters *and/but can/can't* write good
> reports. *He/She can/can't* use computers.
> .... *likes/doesn't* like
> people *and/but can/can't* talk to people on
> the phone.

✔ Quick Check

A Complete the questions or answers.

1. Why do you like your job? ....
   the money is good.
2. .... do .... like the phone?
   Because I like people.
3. Why .... you use a computer?
   .... it'..... quick.

B Complete the responses. Which *can* (1–4) has a different meaning from the other three?

1. Can you see my car?
   Yes, I .... It's over there.
2. Can you come on Saturday?
   No, I .... Sorry.
3. Can you open the window, please?
   Yes, sure. .... that OK?
4. Can you write in English?
   Yes, ...

B   WORK IN OTHER COUNTRIES

1 Jobs in other countries?   vocabulary

In your country, which of these people can find good jobs in other countries?

student · soldier · manager · engineer · nurse

doctor · teacher · waiter · shop assistant

Have you got a friend with a job in another country?

Read these questions and write one more question.

With a partner, ask and answer the questions about your friend.

> Where is he/she?
> What's his/her job?
> Is he/she happy?
> Is the salary good?
> ....(Write your question.)

---

2 Change is good, because ...

◀ John Grant works in an international bank. He's 25, not married, and lives in Geneva.

Mary O'Malley is 38 and teaches ▶
English part-time in Italy. She has
a young son and her husband is
a writer of travel books.

Which person likes change, do you think? John or Mary?

Read the things they say.

Today the world is small and many people work in other countries. Do they like change? John and Mary write:

I like change, it's good. I like my job in Switzerland because in a new country I can learn new things. I can see new places and that's interesting. I can work with new technology, new ideas, new people. In today's world it's important to like change because change is everywhere – in work, in sport, in families. You can't live in the past because there isn't time.

I don't like a lot of change. I'm a teacher and my students here in Italy are very important. I like time to understand my students – to learn about their lives and to be their friend and guide. I like to visit new countries because it's exciting, but I like lots of time to understand the life of the people in other countries. I haven't got a lot of things or a lot of money. I like to give time to the people in my life because they are my life.

Answer the questions. Choose *one* good reason (1–5) for John, and one good reason (1–5) for Mary.

Does John like change? .... Why?
1. Because it's interesting.
2. Because he's 25.
3. Because he isn't married.
4. Because he's a man.
5. .... (Write your reason.)

Does Mary like change? .... Why not?
1. Because she's a teacher.
2. Because she likes time to learn about people and places.
3. Because she's 38.
4. Because she has a young son.
5. .... (Write your reason.)

Talk about your two reasons, like this:

I think John likes change because ...
(Perhaps) Mary doesn't like change because ...

What about you? Do you like change? Why? Why not?

Is change exciting, interesting or difficult for you?

HELP	In your language?
It's hard to say.	....
It's difficult to know.	....

3 International job applications

reading; listening for present tense; impersonal *you*

Think about job applications and interviews in your profession in your country.
Tick the boxes and/or add words.

1. ☐ You see an advert in the newspaper.

HELP	In your language?
usually	....
a long time	....

2. ☐ You phone to talk about the job and ask for an application form.

☐ You write for an application form.
☐ You write ...

3. You send the application form ...

☐ with a photo.　☐ with no photo.　☐ with ....

4. The company says ...

☐ no interview.　☐ go for an interview.

5. You go for an interview with ...

☐ one or two people.　☐ four or five people.　☐ .... people.

6. In the interview ...

☐ you talk about salary.　☐ you don't talk about salary.

7. You wait for ...

☐ a week.　☐ two or three weeks.　☐ .... weeks.

8. You get ...

☐ a letter.　☐ a phone call.　☐ ....

▭▭ Listen to two people, one from Australia and one from Ecuador. What happens in their countries? Write three things for each country. Talk with a partner about your three things.

4 Replying to a job advert

simple letter writing

Complete this letter for one of the adverts.

THE AUSTRALIAN *14th May*

Senior Manager
required for import-export company in Hong Kong.

Apply to: Personnel Officer,
Position 145H, Global International,
Box 3421, Hong Kong.

The Independent　28th August

LECTURER
required for computing faculty, private technical university, Bahrein.

Apply in writing to:
Secretary to the Dean,
Faculty of Computing,
Great Western University,
Saskatchewan, Canada.

Dear Sir/Madam,

　　Please send me an application form for the position of .... ,
as advertised in the ....
on ....

　　I look forward to hearing from you,

　　Yours faithfully,

A Study sentences a–d. Answer questions 1–4.

Sentences
a. Things change a lot.
b. They like change.
c. Change is good.
d. A quick change saves time.

Questions
1. In which sentences is change a noun?
   (Sentences ...., ... and ....)
2. In which sentence is change a verb?
   (Sentence ....)
3. In which sentence is change the object?
   (Sentence ....)
4. In which sentences is change the subject?
   (Sentences .... and ....)

B Write words for each definition.

1. You see a job advert and write a letter to get this. (an a........................ f..............)
2. A word for a job in formal letters. (a p..........................)
3. Money you get month by month for professional work. (your s..................)
4. There are many in a newspaper – for jobs, for things in the shops for example. (a..................s)

C EXCUSES, EXCUSES

1 In conversation | saying why you can't do something; pronunciation: stressed syllables |

▭▭ Listen to the conversation and mark some of the strong sounds, like this:

Example: *Can you come to a pãrty on Sãturday ẽvening?*

A: Can you come to a party on Saturday evening?
B: Where?
A: Our place.
B: Is it your birthday?
A: No ... Eva's.
B: Oh, er, sorry, I can't. I haven't got the car.
A: What about the bus?
B: There aren't any buses on Saturday ... and I'm really busy with a job application.
A: Oh, OK. See you.
B: Bye. Say Happy Birthday to Eva.

How many excuses are there in the conversation?

Have conversations with a partner. Here is some help.

Partner A:
Can you come for a meal this evening?
What about Saturday evening?

Excuses for Partner B:
I'm sorry, I can't ...
    I'm very busy/tired.
    I haven't got time.
    my father is here.
    my daughter is ill.

2 Record and write | writing your recorded conversation |

Can you record your conversation?

Listen to your conversation and write all the words.

Ask your teacher for help.

3 I'm sorry but ... | listening for excuses |

A   ☐   B   ☐   C   ☐

D   ☐   E   ☐   F   ☐   G   ☐

 Listen. Look at the pictures and tick the excuses they talk about.

Your manager asks:

– Can you work this evening?
– Can you come to the office on Sunday?

What do you say?

HELP	In your language?
I'm unemployed.	....
I am the manager.	....
I say *No*.	....

✔ Quick Check

A You are a secretary for Sofia, Carlos, John and Mary. Complete the excuses for them.

1. Can Sofia come to the party on Sunday?
   Sorry .... 's busy, and .... son's ill.
2. Can Carlos come to the office on Saturday?
   Sorry, ... ' s not well and .... car's in Barcelona.
3. Can John and Mary come to Sven's birthday party this evening?
   Sorry, but .... 're in Oslo this weekend with .... mother.

B Write the words for the two conversations in the right order.

1. A: you come at a meeting to the office Can?
   B: is meeting the When?
   A: Friday It's on.
   B: but I'm sorry it's a Friday on holiday.
2. A: an There's dinner on important Friday.
   B: Where it is?
   A: the Greek At restaurant.
   B: my mother is sorry but I'm ill.

PERSONAL STUDY WORKBOOK

- job and business crossword
- reading – job ads
- listening for *because* answers
- visual dictionary – offices and jobs
- reading – episode 11 of *Lost in time*

REVIEW OF UNIT 9

1 On the phone   vocabulary; speaking

bike

You want to sell one of these things:

your first computer   an old car   a bike

Write notes about: the colour, the age and the price.

Now work with another learner.

Partner A: You want to buy something from the other person. Ask questions about the colour, the age and the price. Find out B's address.
Partner B: Answer A's questions about your computer, your car or your bike. Ask when A can come and collect it.

Now change roles.

2 Find the words   vocabulary

Fill the gaps in these sentences. Then put the answer words into the puzzle.

1. Can I pay by credit ....? (4)

2. How .... are those shoes? (4)

3. Fresh or cold food is here. (6)

4. One child, two .... (8)

5. You write with a .... (3)

6. Trousers. They are often blue. (5)

7. How much does this TV ....? (4)

8. Children play with .... (4)

9. A money word, for example, francs, pesetas. (8)

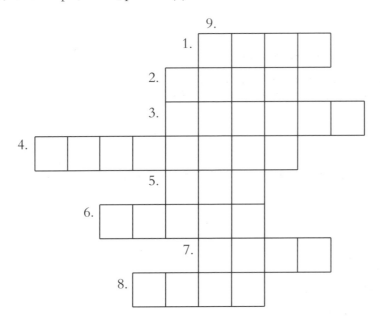

3 Strong or weak sounds [pronunciation]

A 🔊 Do these words sound strong or weak? Listen and write *S* or *W*.

1. *Have*
a. **Have** you got a T-shirt?   b. Yes, we **have**.   c. Can I **have** these cassettes?

2. *Can*
Can I have this necklace please?

3. *There*
Is **there** a black T-shirt?

4. *For*
a. Who's it **for**?   b. It's a souvenir **for** my daughter.

B Which words sound like these words?

1. phone	....	....	all	boss	clock	
2. you	....	....	code	do	floor	
3. cost	....	....	how	know	school	
4. your	....	....	thousand			
5. town	....	....				

🔊 Listen and check your answers.

REVIEW OF UNIT 10

1 Your free time   [present simple; frequency adverbs]

What do you *always*, *usually* or *sometimes* do in your free time? Fill in the table. Follow the examples.

	always	*usually*	*sometimes*
1. in the evening	*have dinner*	*watch TV*	*see friends*
2. at the weekend	....	....	....
3. at parties	....	....	....
4. on holiday	....	....	....

Talk about your free time with another learner.

Example: A: *I usually watch television in the evenings. What about you?*
          B: *I sometimes watch television, but I usually see my friends.*

2 MORning   [stress]

These words all have two parts. Where is the stress? On the first part or the second part?

Example: *mor | ning – MORning*

1. off | ice   2. ye | llow
3. ho | tel   4. post | card
5. ear | ly   6. a | gain
7. wea | ther   8. re | peat

🔊 Listen and check your answers.

12

LET'S HAVE A PARTY

> Language focus:
> suggestions: *Let's ... What about ...?*
> saying *yes* and *no* to suggestions
> *here/there*
>
> Vocabulary:
> parties

A MAKING PLANS

1 Places for a party   speaking; vocabulary

Where is a good place for a party? Here are some ideas.

Write a list of good and bad things about these places, like this:

Place	Good things	Bad things
hotel	bar, disco, waiters	expensive, hot, small
garden	....	....
house or flat	....	....
beach	....	....

Where's the best place for a party? Tell another person your ideas.

2 Decisions   making suggestions; listening and speaking

A 📼 Listen to a conversation between two people. Answer the questions.

1. Who are the two people?
2. Why do they want a party?

B 📼 Listen to the rest of the same conversation. Answer the questions.

1. When do they decide to have the party? Which day? What time?
2. Where do they decide to have their party? Why? Choose one of these places: the beach, a hotel, a student's flat.
3. What is the problem with the other places?

Suggestions	Answers	
	Yes	*No*
Let's have a party.	Great/Good idea.	No.
What about the beach?	OK.	No, it's too cold.

3 Your plans   `speaking`

Work in groups of three or four. Plan a business meeting. Think about:

- the best place: a conference room in a hotel, a bar or café, a small office
- the best day and time

✓ Quick Check

A Say *yes* to these suggestions.

1. Let's have a party at the weekend.
2. What about a beach holiday?
3. Let's go to the swimming pool this afternoon.

Say *no* to these suggestions.

4. What about a holiday in the United States?
5. Let's fly.
6. What about a tour of Australia?

B Fill the gaps in this conversation with one of these words.

about   cold   early   idea   interesting   let's
when   where

A: Let's have a holiday together.
B: That's a good (1) .... Where?
A: What (2) .... the Bahamas?
B: No, that's too expensive for me. (3)
.... go to Norway.
A: No, the weather's too (4) .... in
Norway. What about Australia?

B: OK, there are lots of (5) ....
places to visit there. But (6) ....
in Australia? It's a very big country.
A: What about Tasmania?
B: OK. And (7) ....?
A: March?
B: No, that's too (8) .... Let's go
in May.
A: OK.

C Fill the gaps in these sentences with one of these words.

at   for   in   of   with

1. What about a holiday .... August?
2. I'd like a hotel .... a swimming pool.
3. Let's have a drink in the bar .... the hotel.
4. My university course finishes .... the end
of next month.
5. Summer in Istanbul is too hot .... me.

B INVITATIONS

1 Sending invitations   `reading and writing`

Here is the invitation for Mayumi's and Satoshi's end-of-course party. Fill in the details.

Write an invitation to your party.
Copy this invitation or make your own.

To ....
Bring a friend.
Come to Satoshi's and Mayumi's
end-of-course party
On ....
Time ....
Place ....
Please bring something to drink or
something to eat.

Can you come?
Don't forget to tell us.
Phone Satoshi – 987891

---

2 Can you come?   [listening]

A 🎧 Listen to five phone conversations. Who can come to the party? Who can't come? Who doesn't know?

Write ✓, ✗ or ? next to the names.

1. Cecile ☐   2. John ☐   3. Peter ☐   4. Maria ☐   5. Lucy ☐

🎧 Listen again. Who can bring a friend? What are the friends' names?

B Here are parts of the conversations. Fill the spaces with one of these words or phrases.

listen	a pity	perhaps	probably	sorry	sure

1. SATOSHI: John, this is Satoshi. Can you come to the party next Friday?
   JOHN: No, I can't. ....
   SATOSHI: Oh, that's ....

2. PETER: Mayumi! How are you?
   MAYUMI: I'm fine. ...., can you come to our party on Friday?
   PETER: I'm not .... I'm very busy this week. ....

3. MAYUMI: Can you come to the party on Friday?
   LUCY: I don't really know. ....

🎧 Listen to these conversations again and check your answers.

3 On the phone   [speaking]

Sit back to back with another learner and have phone conversations.

A
Ask: 'Can you come to my party?'
Say where.
Say which day.
Say what time.

B
Ask about the place.
Ask about the day.
Ask about the time.
Answer *yes*, *no* or *not sure*.

Now change roles.

4 Food and drink   [speaking]

Talk to another person about things to get for the party. Think about:

– things to eat; – things to drink; – music; – other things.

Which things have you got already? Write a shopping list of things you haven't got.

✔ Quick Check

A Answer these invitations.

1. Can you come to the party next weekend?
   (Say *yes*.)
2. Can you come to the cinema on Monday?
   (Say *no* and then say why you can't.)
3. Can you come for lunch tomorrow?
   (Say *not sure* and give a reason.)
4. Can you come to the international conference in Paris? (Say *yes*.)
5. Do you want to go on holiday in August?
   (Say *no* and give a reason.)

B Correct these expressions. Some have a word missing and some have an extra word.

1. Can I speak John, please?
2. Yes, in one moment.
3. Hello, Eva is speaking.
4. Hello, is Maria?
5. Hi, it Mayumi here.
6. Hello, Raymundo, is Mayumi.

C THE PARTY

1 Conversations [listening]

📼 Here are some groups of people at Satoshi's and Mayumi's party. What are they talking about? Listen to their conversations. Tick the subjects.

Subjects	Conversation	1	2	3	4
home countries		....	....	....	....
food or drink		....	....	....	....
music		....	....	....	....
jobs		....	....	....	....

HELP	In your language?
famous for	....
different from	....
here	....
there	....

Raymundo

Pascal

Karen Cecile

Mayumi Tran Lucy

Satoshi Peter

Maria Manuel Eva Nicole

2 Party talk   speaking

Think of five questions to ask people at a party. Write them down.

Examples: *Where are you from?*
          What do you do there?

Give yourself a new character. Think of a new name, a new country, a new job, etc.

You are at a party. Talk to other learners. Ask your questions and answer their questions.

3 Hi from Mexico!   reading and writing

Two weeks after the end-of-course party, everyone is in their own country again. Here are two postcards to Satoshi and Mayumi.

Fill the gaps in the postcards with one of these words.

Postcard 1: come   country   fantastic   friends   home   music   party   thank

Postcard 2: course   friend   party   next   nice   number   write

1

Hi from Mexico,
We're (1) .... again after a great time.
The English course was (2) ....
We really miss all our (3) ....
Your end-of-course (4) .... was wonderful – the food, the (5) ....,
the people. (6) .... you for everything.
Say a big hello to all our friends.
(7) .... and see us when you are in our (8) ....
Love from
Raymundo and Karen

2

To Satoshi, Mayumi and all our friends,
How are you all? I start work again here tomorrow with my Dutch friends. It's (1) .... to see them, but I miss everyone on the English (2) ....
My best (3) .... Nicole is in America again now, but she wants to come home (4) .... month.
Please phone or (5) .... to me.
You know my phone (6) .... and my address.
Thanks again for the fantastic (7) ....
See you soon.
Love
Eva

Write your own postcard like these to a friend in another country.

✔ Quick Check

A Write the long forms.

1. I'm really pleased you're here.
2. How's your father?
3. I haven't got anything, I'm afraid.

B Write the short forms.

1. Let us go shopping.
2. My friend Nicole is in America now.
3. Come and see us when you are in Mexico.
4. I would like to come home soon.

C Match the questions with the short answers. There is an extra answer.

1. Where are you from?	a. No.
2. Are you Italian?	b. Twenty-three.
3. How's your brother?	c. Twenty pounds.
4. What kind of food is it?	d. OK.
5. What's this?	e. Argentina.
6. How old are you?	f. Probably.
7. How much is it?	g. Italian.
	h. French wine.

D Now make the short answers longer.

Example: *Short*   *Longer*
         Argentina   *From Argentina* or
                      I'm from Argentina.

PERSONAL STUDY WORKBOOK

• listening to people organising a party
• reading and writing party invitations
• making telephone conversations
• pronunciation work
• visual dictionary – let's have a party
• reading – episode 12 of *Lost in time*

D   REVIEW AND DEVELOPMENT

REVIEW OF UNIT 10

1 Whose clothes? | *whose*; vocabulary |

Whose clothes are these? You decide. Match the three people with the clothes.

Now talk to another learner. Ask and answer questions, like this:

A: *Whose jeans are these?*   B: *I think they're Pat's.*

2 Compliments speaking

Friends and people in your family have some new things. Say you like them.
Use *I like ...; ... suit(s) you; ... look(s) lovely.*

1. Your sister has a new white blouse.
2. Your best friend has a new necklace.
3. Your partner has some new green jeans.
4. Your boss has a new fast car.
5. Your mother has some new earrings.
6. Your teacher has some new shoes.

Talk to other learners. Tell them what you like.

REVIEW OF UNIT 11

1 Quick conversations listening; pronunciation

A Listen to six conversations. Do you hear *can, do* or *does*? Do you hear *she, he* or *they*?

	1	2	3	4	5	6		1	2	3	4	5	6
Can							he						
Do							she						
Does							they						

B Listen to the two *Can ...?* questions again with short answers.
Has the *a* in *can/can't* got:

the sound /ə/?   the sound /æ/?   the sound /ɑː/?
1. Can he go to Barcelona? No, he can't.
2. Can she phone Monika at nine? Yes, she can.

Practise the questions and answers in pairs.

2 Can your mother drive? Can/Do/Does ...? speaking

Which verbs in Box A go with *Can ...?* questions?

Box A	speak English	like Italian food	eat hot food
	eat meat	speak French	speak German
	sing well	drive	like holidays

Box B	your parents	your brother	your sister	your mother	your friends
	your father	your manager	your husband	your wife	you

Ask and answer *Can/Do/Does ...?* questions. Use language from *A* and *B*.

Examples: A: *Can (Do) your parents speak English?*
B: *Yes, they can./No, they can't./Yes, they can, a bit.*
(Yes they do, with English visitors.)
A: *Can your mother drive?*
B: *No, she can't./Yes, she can.*

HELP	In your language?
Yes, of course.	....
Yes, a bit.	....

GRAMMAR REFERENCE
Useful lists

Alphabet

Aa	Bb	Cc	Dd	Ee	Ff	Gg
Hh	Ii	Jj	Kk	Ll	Mm	Nn
Oo	Pp	Qq	Rr	Ss	Tt	Uu
Vv	Ww	Xx	Yy	Zz		

Numbers

Cardinal numbers 1–10

one	1	six	6	zero	0 (or 'o')
two	2	seven	7		
three	3	eight	8		
four	4	nine	9		
five	5	ten	10		

Note:

We say *double ...* for two numbers in telephone numbers.
Examples:
double six = 66   double four = 44

Cardinal numbers 11–30

eleven	11	sixteen	16	twenty-one	21
twelve	12	seventeen	17	twenty-two	22
thirteen	13	eighteen	18	twenty-three	23
fourteen	14	nineteen	19	twenty-nine	29
fifteen	15	twenty	20	thirty	30

Cardinal numbers 31–100

thirty-one	31	seventy	70
forty	40	eighty	80
fifty	50	ninety	90
sixty	60	a hundred	100

Ordinal numbers: first – tenth

1	one	one man	the **first** man
2	two	two children	the **second** child
3	three	three letters	the **third** letter
4	four	four buildings	the **fourth** building
5	five	five floors	the **fifth** floor
6	six	six visitors	the **sixth** visitor
7	seven	seven stations	the **seventh** station
8	eight	eight mornings	the **eighth** morning
9	nine	nine days	the **ninth** day
10	ten	ten taxis	the **tenth** taxi

Large numbers: 100–1,000,000

100	**a hundred**/**one** hundred
135	**a**/**one** hundred **and** thirty-five
376	**three hundred** and seventy-six [NOT ~~three hundreds~~]
1,000	**a thousand**/**one** thousand
1,104	**one** thousand, **one** hundred and four [NOT ~~a thousand~~]
32,423	thirty-two thousand, four hundred and twenty-three
461,534	four hundred and sixty-one thousand, five hundred and thirty-four
1,000,000	**a million**/**one** million
1,000,017	**one** million and seventeen
1,547,982	one million, five hundred and forty-seven thousand, nine hundred and eighty-two

The time

08.00	eight o'clock (in the morning)
09.05	five past nine
10.10	ten past ten
11.15	a quarter past eleven/eleven fifteen
12.00	twelve o'clock/midday
12.20	twenty past twelve
13.30	half past one/one thirty
16.35	twenty-five to five (in the afternoon)
20.40	twenty to nine (in the evening)
22.45	a quarter to eleven (in the evening/at night)
23.50	ten to twelve (at night)/ten to midnight
00.00	twelve o'clock/midnight
03.00	three o'clock (in the morning)

Days of the week

Sunday   Monday   Tuesday   Wednesday
Thursday   Friday   Saturday

Months

January   February   March   April   May   June
July   August   September   October   November
December

Personal pronouns

1 PERSON THING	2 + PERSONS/THINGS
I	we
you	you
he	
she	they
it	

Pronouns with *be* (*am/is/are*)

SHORT FORM	LONG FORM
I'm ten (10).	I am ten.

You're ten.   You are ten.

He's ten.   He is ten.

She's ten.   She is ten.

It's ten.   It is ten.

We're ten.   We are ten.

They're ten.   They are ten.

Questions and answers with *are/am*

Are you John?	Yes, I am. (NOT ~~Yes, I'm.~~)
	No, I'm not.
Am I late?	Yes, you are. (NOT ~~Yes, you're.~~)
	No, you're not.

Questions and answers with *How ...?*

SHORT FORM	LONG FORM	ANSWER
	How are you?	I'm fine. (or Fine.)
How's Joanna?	How is Joanna?	She's fine.
How's she?	How is she?	She's fine.
How's he?	How is he?	He's fine.
	How is it?	It's fine.
	How are you?	I'm fine./We're fine.
	How are they?	I'm fine, how about you?
		I'm fine, thanks.
		They're fine.

This in introductions

*Hello. I'm John and **this** is Kate.*
*Hi. I'm Joanna and **this** is John.*

Mr/Ms/Mrs

married   not married   married or not married

Examples:
Mr Smith   Ms Lopez   Mrs Tanaka

Hello, goodbye and thank you

FORMAL	INFORMAL
Hello.	Hi.
Goodbye.	Bye./Bye bye.
Thank you.	Thanks.

2

Questions and answers with *is*

QUESTIONS		ANSWERS
SHORT FORM	LONG FORM	
What's this?	What is this?	It's a hotel.
What's that?	What is that?	It's the hotel.
Where's the hotel	Where is the hotel?	It's in New York.
	Is it a hotel?	Yes, it is.
		No, it isn't.

This and *that*

This is the bar.

That's the sauna.

The plural words for *this* and *that* are *these* and *those*.

SINGULAR	PLURAL
this restaurant	**these** restaurants
that man	**those** men

Articles: *a* and *the*

*It's **a** hotel.* – We don't know which hotel. We don't know its name.
*It's **the** Hilton Hotel.* – We know the name of the hotel.

Plural nouns

1. noun + s	name/name**s**, student/student**s**
2. –x/–s/–ch/–sh + es	box/box**es**, bus/bus**es**
3. –y changes to –ies	city/cit**ies**, country/countr**ies**
4. irregular	man/**men**, woman/**women**, person/**people**

Possessive adjectives

I	**my**
you	**your**

This is **my** room.

That's **your** room.

Possessive adjectives

My/your (See Unit 2.)

his	It's **his** restaurant.	**His** restaurant is nice.
her	It's **her** restaurant.	**Her** restaurant is nice.
its	This is **its** drink.	**Its** drink is in the kitchen.

their   It's **their** restaurant.   **Their** restaurant is nice.

Note:
Its drink (possessive adjective)
It's my drink. (it is = it's)

Question forms with *is/are* and answers

QUESTIONS	ANSWERS
Is he busy?	Yes, he is. No, he isn't. (long answer: No, he is not.)
Is she popular?	Yes, she is. No, she isn't. (No, she is not.)
Is it nice?	Yes, it is. No, it isn't. (No, it is not.)
Are they nice?	Yes, they are. No, they aren't. (No, they are not.)

Where ... from? questions and answers

SHORT QUESTION	LONG QUESTION
Where's he from?	Where is he from?
SHORT ANSWER	LONG ANSWER
France.	He is from France. He's from France. From France.
SHORT QUESTION	LONG QUESTION
–	Where are they from?
SHORT ANSWER	LONG ANSWER
London.	They are from London. They're from London. From London.

How old ...? questions and answers

How old is he?	Fifteen. He's fifteen. He is fifteen.
How old are you?	Ten. I'm ten. I am ten.
How old are they?	Twenty. They're twenty. They are twenty.

Adjectives

Examples:
good   nice   popular   old   small

He is a good man.   *He is good.*
She is a good woman.   *She is good.*
They are good men.   *They are good.*
Good men are popular.

a and an

a
Examples:
a name   a man   a woman   a restaurant   a friend   a ring
a nice earring   a good address
an
Examples:
an address   an earring   an umbrella
an Indian ring   an old man
An is with words with a first letter: a, e, i, o, u.

there is/there are

LONG FORM
There is a restaurant in the hotel.
There are restaurants in the hotel.

SHORT FORM
There's a restaurant in the hotel.

QUESTIONS
Is there a restaurant in the hotel?
Are there restaurants in the hotel?

ANSWERS
Yes, there is. (~~Yes, there's.~~)
No, there isn't.

Yes, there are.
No, there aren't.

Is there ...?/Are there ...?

Singular
QUESTION
Is there a cinema in your town?

SHORT ANSWERS
Yes, **there is.**
No, **there isn't.**

Plural
QUESTION
Are there any banks in your town?

SHORT ANSWERS
Yes, **there are**.
No, **there aren't**.

Use *any* not *a/an* in questions.
Example:
*Are there **any** hotels in your town?*

Perhaps/I think

He's American.   I know this. I am sure.
***Perhaps/I think** he's American.* I don't know. I'm not sure.

has got/have got

SHORT FORM	LONG FORM	NEGATIVE
I've got	I have got	I haven't got
You've got	You have got	You haven't got
She's/He's/It's got	She/He/It has got	She/He/It hasn't got
We've/They've got	We/They have got	We/They haven't got

Examples:
I've got a car.   *They've got a coffee shop.*
It's got a kitchen.   *She hasn't got a sister.*

Note:
It's got = it has got (NOT ~~it is got~~)

Questions and answers with *have got*

Have you got a manager?   Yes, I have. (~~Yes, I've.~~)/
                            No, I haven't.

Has she/he got a car?   Yes, she/he has./
                            No, she/he hasn't.

Has it got an airport?   Yes, it has./No, it hasn't.
Have we/they got a drink?   Yes, we/they have./
                            No, we/they haven't.

What have you got?   I've got a coffee.
What has it got?   It's got a bedroom.
  (short form: What's it got?)
How many (brothers) have you got? I've got two.

some and any

any *in questions*
Have you got any coffee?   Have you got any tablets?

some *in answers/statements*
Yes, I've got some (coffee).   There's some coffee in the kitchen.

any *in answers/statements*
No. I haven't got any (coffee/tablets).   There isn't any coffee.

Imperative form of verbs

Examples:
Go to bed!
Come to Paris.
Tell your mother.
Call your manager.
Phone your sister.

Imperative: negative form

SHORT FORM	LONG FORM
Don't go to bed.	Do not go to bed.
Don't come to Paris.	Do not come to Paris.
Don't tell your mother.	Do not tell your mother.
Don't call your manager.	Do not call your manager.
Don't phone your sister.	Do not phone your sister.

GRAMMAR REFERENCE

Prepositions (i)

to: *Go to bed.*
at: *Stay at the hotel. Stay at home.*
for: *Stay for one day.*

Prepositions (ii)

Present simple verbs

Use present simple verbs for routines – what you do every day, every week, every month, etc.

STATEMENTS		NEGATIVE STATEMENTS	
I		I	
You	**work** here.	You	**don't work** there.
We		We	
They		They	
He		He	
She	**works** here.	She	**doesn't work** there.
(It)		(It)	

Wh- questions

Where	**do**	you they	**work**?
When	**does**	he she	**get up**?

Yes/No questions

Do	you they		
		work	in Istanbul?
Does	he she		

Short answers

	I/we		
Yes,	you	**do**.	
	they		
	he		
	she	**does**.	
	I/we		
No,	you/they		**don't**.
	he/she		**doesn't**.

Other verbs

Endings	I/you, etc.	he/she
–ly/–ry = + –ies	fly, carry	**flies, carries**
But	buy, stay, pay	**buys, stays, pays**
–ch/–sh/–s = + –es	watch, wash, guess	**watches, washes, guesses**
–o = + –es	go, do	**goes, does**

Verb tenses: Present simple

1 PERSON/THING	2 + PERSONS/THINGS
I like	We like
You like	You like
She/he/it likes	They like

Examples:
I like coffee.	*We like New York.*
She likes tea.	*They like their manager.*

SHORT FORM	LONG FORM
I don't like	I do not like
We don't like	We do not like
You don't like	You do not like
She/he/it doesn't like	She/he/it does not like
They don't like	They do not like

Examples:
I don't like hotels.	*They don't like tea.*
She doesn't like my sister.	

Questions and answers: present simple *like*

QUESTIONS	ANSWERS
Do you like ...?	Yes, I do./No, I don't.
Does she/he/it like ...?	Yes, she/he/it does./ No, she/he/it doesn't.
Do we like ...?	Yes, we do./No, we don't.
Do they like ...?	Yes, they do./No, they don't.

Agreeing

I like coffee.	*So do I./Me too.*
She/he likes tea.	*So does he/she.*
	So do we.
	So do they.

Question forms with *How long ...?* and *How many ...?*

How long is your course?
How many days are there in June?
How many men are there in this room?

The word after *How many ...?* is always a plural countable noun, for example day**s**, cit**ies**, restaurant**s**.

Conjunctions *and* and *but*

I like coffee and I like tea. (I like the two drinks – coffee/tea.)
I like coffee and tea.

I like coffee but I don't like tea. (I like one drink – coffee.)
I like coffee but not tea.

How much ...?

Use *How much ...?* to ask about prices.

QUESTIONS			ANSWERS
How much is	that wallet?		**It's** ten pounds.
are	those shoes?		**They're** three pounds.

How much does	that wallet	**cost**?	**It costs** five dollars.
do	those shoes		**They cost** thirty dollars.

Would like

I'd like / I would like = I want. It's polite.

STATEMENTS
I'd	**like**	a coffee,	please.
We'd		sandwiches,	

QUESTIONS
Would you like a coffee?

SHORT ANSWERS
Yes, (please) **I would**./
Yes, please.
No, thanks./No, thank you.

10

Always, usually, often, sometimes, never

Use these words with present simple verbs. They answer the question *How often ...?*

I/you/we/they	**always**	go to work on Friday.
	usually	get up early.
He/she	**often**	goes to work on Friday.
	sometimes	gets up early.

always = 100% / every day
usually = 80–90% / 5–6 days a week
often = 50–80% / 4–5 days a week
sometimes = 20–50% / 1–3 days a week
never = 0%/0 days a week

Possessive 's

Use *'s* with names or nouns.

Examples:
John has got a car.   *This is **John's car**/his car.*
Jenny has got blue jeans.   *These are **Jenny's jeans**/ her jeans.*

The nurse has a uniform.   *This is the **nurse's** uniform/ her uniform.*

Whose?

Use *whose* to ask questions about possessions.

QUESTIONS	ANSWERS
Whose car is this?	It's John's car.
	It's John's.
Whose shoes are these?	They're Monica's shoes.
	They're Monica's.

Which?

Use *which* with nouns to ask about things or places.

QUESTIONS	ANSWERS
Which car is John's?	The red car (is John's).
Which shoes would you like?	I'd like the white shoes.

too

Use *too* with adjectives to describe nouns. Something is not right.

Example:
*This cap is **too small** for me.* (My head is big.)

Use *too* with adverbs to talk about verbs.

Example:
*Don't walk **too quickly**.* (I'm tired.)

can/can't (ability)

I can (write).   We can (write).
You can (write).
She/He/It can (write).   They can (write).

Note:

Can is used with the infinitive of the verb. Examples of infinitives: *write, eat, come, read.*

Examples:
I can write good letters.   She can read Spanish reports.
They can come to the meeting.

Negative

SHORT FORM	LONG FORM
I can't (write).	I cannot (write).
You can't (write).	You cannot (write).
She/he/it can't (write).	She/he/it cannot (write).
We can't (write).	We cannot (write).
They can't (write).	They cannot (write).

Examples:
He can't come to the restaurant.   They can't use a computer.
We can't write business letters.   I can't see your car.

Questions and answers with can

QUESTIONS	ANSWERS
Can you come?	Yes, I can./No, I can't.
Can she/he/it speak Turkish?	Yes, she/he/it can./ No, she/he/it can't.
Can we read Italian newspapers?	Yes, we can./ No, we can't.
Can they write good letters?	Yes, they can./ No, they can't.

Questions and answers with Why (not)? and because

QUESTIONS	ANSWERS
Why are you tired?	(I'm tired) because it's 12 o'clock at night.
You can't see the manager. Why not?	Because he's not in his office today.
I like France. Why?	Because French people are interesting.
Why do you like coffee?	Because it's tasty.
Why has he got your car?	Because his car is at the garage.

Impersonal you

> ### What to do?
>
> You phone the manager and leave your name, then you write an application.
>
> You get a reply in one week.

You here means any person or every person, NOT one person, for example YOU.

12

Suggestions

MAKING SUGGESTIONS	ANSWERING SUGGESTIONS	
	POSITIVE	NEGATIVE
Let's have a drink.	Great/Good idea.	No.
What about a coffee?	OK.	I'd like a tea.

Here and there

Here means this place. *There* means that place.

Examples:
*My house is **here**. **This** is my house.* (I am in or near my house.)
*Your house is **there**. **That's** your house.* (We are not near your house.)

Here and *there* also mean *to this place* and *to that place.*

Examples:
*Come **here**. I want to talk to you.*
*Don't go **there**. It's a terrible school.*

I'm here and you're there.

No, **I'm** here and **you're** there.

TAPESCRIPTS

UNIT 1

Lesson A Hello, am I late?

Exercise 1B
1. Hello, Juan.
2. Good morning. I'm Gloria Jones.
3. Hi, nice day.
4. Hi, Maria. How are you?
5. Hello, I'm Jill Smith. Are you Kemal Caglar?

Exercise 1C
1. WOMAN: Good morning. I'm Gloria Jones.
   PEOPLE: Morning.
2. WOMAN: Hi, nice day.
   MAN: Oh, hi, yes ... beautiful.
3. RYOKO: Hello, Juan.
   JUAN: Hello, Ryoko.
4. JILL: Hello, I'm Jill Smith. Are you Kemal Caglar?
   KEMAL: Yes, pleased to meet you.
5. PHIL: Hi, Maria. How are you?
   MARIA: Hi, Phil, fine, thanks.

Exercise 2
1. JUAN: Hello, I'm Juan. Pleased to meet you.
   PATRICIA: Hello, pleased to meet you. I'm Patricia.
2. WOMAN: Hi, how are you?
   MAN: Hello, fine, thanks, and you?
   WOMAN: Fine, thanks.

Exercise 3
1. WOMAN: Are you Ms Tanaka?
   MS TANAKA: Yes, I am. Am I late?
   WOMAN: No.
   MS TANAKA: Good.
2. WOMAN: Are you Mr James?
   MR JAMES: Yes, I am. Am I late?
   WOMAN: Yes, you are.
   MR JAMES: I'm sorry.
3. MAN: Are you Mrs Petrovna?
   MRS SUKOVA: No, I'm not, I'm Mrs Irina Sukova.
                Am I late?
   MAN: No, you're not.
   MRS SUKOVA: Oh, good.

Exercise 4
1. JACQUES: Hello I'm Jacques Leotard; this is Maria Gasso.
2. WOMAN: What's your name?
   JACQUES: I'm Jacques Leotard and this is Maria Gasso.
3. JACQUES: Hi, I'm Jacques, this is Maria.
   PEOPLE AT BARBECUE: Hi!

Lesson B How are you?

Exercise 1
1. WOMAN: Hello, how are you?
   MAN: Hello, I'm fine, thanks.
2. WOMAN 1: Hello, how are you?
   WOMAN 2: Hello, I'm OK, thanks.
3. WOMAN: Hello, how are you?
   MAN: Hi, all right, thanks.
4. WOMAN 1: Hello, how are you?
   WOMAN 2: Hello, not bad, thank you.

Exercise 2
Example
MAN: How's Vesna?
WOMAN: She's fine.
1. MAN: How's Vesna?
   WOMAN: She's fine.
2. MAN: How's Goran?
   WOMAN: He's OK.
3. MAN: How are Anna and Nick?
   WOMAN: They're all right.
4. MAN: How are you and Josef?
   WOMAN: We're fine.
5. MAN: How's the coffee shop?
   WOMAN: It's busy.
6. MAN: How's Brisbane?
   WOMAN: It's beautiful.

Exercise 3C
The names are:
1. Charles Dickens. Spelt CHARLES DICKENS.
2. William Shakespeare Spelt WILLIAM SHAKESPEARE.

Lesson C How about a drink? OK

Exercise 2C
a. A: What's your number?
   B: It's 801 25466.
b. A: What's your number?
   B: It's 635 12449.

c. A: What's your number?
   B: It's 199 72680.
d. What's your number?
   Write your number.

Exercise 3
1. MAN 1:   Thanks, goodbye.
   WOMAN 1: Bye.
2. WOMAN 2: Bye, thanks.
   MAN 2:   Bye bye.
3. MAN 3:   Goodbye and thank you.
   WOMAN 1: Goodbye.
4. WOMAN 3: Bye and thanks for a nice time.
   MAN 2:   You're welcome.

Lesson D Classroom English

Exercise 1
TEACHER: Can you spell 'busy', please? ... er ... Juan.
JUAN: B-U-S-Y.
TEACHER: Good.

TEACHER: Busy. Repeat please, ... er ... Mira.
MIRA: Busy.
TEACHER: Very good. OK ... er ....

TEACHER: Can you write 'busy', please? Good. Listen,
         please. 'Welcome to New York'.
JUAN: Can you write 'welcome', please?
TEACHER: Yes, OK.

Exercise 2A
1. Can you spell 'beautiful'?
2. Can you write 'coffee'?
3. Can you write 'welcome'?
4. Can you spell 'fine'?

Exercise 2B
A: Can you spell 'beautiful'?
B: Yes, 'beautiful', B-E-A-U-T-I-F-U-L.
A: Good.

A: Can you spell 'fine'?
B: Yes, 'fine', F-I-N-E.
A: Very good.

UNIT 2

Lesson A Countries and cities

Exercise 1
1. Good morning, ladies and gentlemen. Welcome to Rio.
   Thank you for flying with Varig Airlines.
2. Hello everybody. I'm Gina – welcome to Rome.
3. Hi! I'm Alexei. We're in Moscow and I'm your guide
   today.
4. Hello and welcome. I'm Jacqueline and I'm from the
   Sheraton Hotel in Istanbul.

Exercise 3
PAUL: Taxi! Taxi!
TAXI DRIVER: Hi. Where to?
SUE: The Plaza Hotel, please.
TAXI DRIVER: The Plaza. Sure
PAUL: Look Sue, the Statue of Liberty.
SUE: It's beautiful! And what's that? Is it the
             Empire State Building?
PAUL: No, it isn't. It's the World Trade Centre.
SUE: Fantastic! Where is the Empire State
             Building?
PAUL: I don't know.
SUE: Is that a station?
TAXI DRIVER: Yeah, it's Penn Station.
SUE: Thanks.
PAUL: That's a nice restaurant.
TAXI DRIVER: Yeah, it's a very popular restaurant.
SUE: Is this Central Park?
TAXI DRIVER: Yeah. That's right.
SUE: Look, the hotel.
PAUL: Great!
TAXI DRIVER: Twenty dollars, please.
PAUL: Thank you.
TAXI DRIVER: Thanks. Have a nice day.
SUE: Bye.

Exercise 4A and 4B
1. Ankara is in Turkey. (Ankara's)
2. Cairo is in Egypt. (Cairo's)
3. Tokyo is in Japan. (Tokyo's)
4. Moscow is in Russia. (Moscow's)
5. Athens is in Greece. (Athens is)
6. Warsaw is in Poland. (Warsaw's)

Lesson B Numbers and addresses

Exercise 1C
twenty twenty-five thirty twelve fourteen sixteen eighteen
eleven thirteen fifteen seventeen nineteen twenty-one
twenty-nine twenty-eight twenty-seven twenty-six twenty-
two twenty-three twenty-four

Exercise 2
1. RECEPTIONIST: What's your address, please, Mr Jones?
   MAN: It's 25, York Avenue Liverpool,
                 L14 2PR.
2. RECEPTIONIST: What's your first name please,
                 Mrs Smith?
   WOMAN: Julie, that's J U L I E.
   RECEPTIONIST: Thank you, and what's your address?
   WOMAN: It's 24, Exeter Gardens, Manchester.
   RECEPTIONIST: Can you spell Exeter, please?
   WOMAN: Yes, that's E X E T E R.
   RECEPTIONIST: Thank you, and what's your post code?
   WOMAN: It's M17 2AG.
   RECEPTIONIST: M7 2AG?
   WOMAN: No, M17.
   RECEPTIONIST: Thanks.
3. RECEPTIONIST: What's your address, please, Mr Procter?
   MAN: Sixteen, New Road, Melbourne.
   RECEPTIONIST: Sixteen?
   MAN: Yes. Sixteen, New Road, Melbourne,
                 3001, Aus ...
   RECEPTIONIST: Three O O one.
   MAN: Yes, that's Australia, of course.
   RECEPTIONIST: Oh, and can you tell me your first
                 name, please?
   MAN: Yes, it's Simon.
   RECEPTIONIST: Is that S I M O N?
   MAN: Yes, that's right.
4. RECEPTIONIST: What's your address, please,
                 Ms Harriman?
   WOMAN: It's 21, Central Avenue, Washington,
                 DC.
   RECEPTIONIST: Twenty-nine, Central Avenue, Wash ...
   WOMAN: Not 29, 21.
   RECEPTIONIST: Sorry.
5. RECEPTIONIST: Can you tell me your address,
                 please, Miss Collins?
   WOMAN: Of course, it's 28, Barrack Street ...
   RECEPTIONIST: Barrack Street? Can you spell
                 that, please?
   WOMAN: Yes, it's B A R R A C K Street.
   RECEPTIONIST: 18, Barrack Street ...
   WOMAN: No, 28
   RECEPTIONIST: Sorry, 28, Barrack Street ...
   WOMAN: Cape Town, eight O O O,
                 South Africa.
   RECEPTIONIST: Thank you.
6. RECEPTIONIST: Can you tell me your first name, please,
                 Mr Charles?
   MAN: Yes, of course, it's William.
   RECEPTIONIST: Can you spell that, please.
   MAN: Yes, W I L L I A M.
   RECEPTIONIST: Thank you. And your address?
   MAN: 18 Park Road, Perth 6026, Western
                 Australia.
   RECEPTIONIST: Perth 18?
   MAN: No, Perth 6026. It's 18 Park Road.
   RECEPTIONIST: Right. Thanks.

Exercise 3A
Version 1
Tenth floor Ninth floor Eighth floor Seventh floor Sixth
floor Fifth floor Fourth floor Third floor Second floor First
floor Ground floor
Version 2
LIFT: Tenth floor.
MAN 1:   Hi.
WOMAN 1: Good morning.
LIFT: Ninth floor.
LIFT: Eighth floor.
MAN 2:   Morning. Nice day.
MAN 1:   Hi.
WOMAN 1: Hello.
LIFT: Seventh floor.
LIFT: Sixth floor.
LIFT: Fifth floor.
WOMAN 2: Hi, Sue. How are you?
WOMAN 1: Fine, thanks. And you?
WOMAN 2: I'm fine.
LIFT: Fourth floor.
MAN 3:   Morning.
OTHERS: Hi. Morning. Hello.
LIFT: Third floor.

LIFT: Second floor.
LIFT: First floor.
LIFT: Ground floor.
ALL: Bye. Goodbye. Bye.

Exercise 3B
RECEPTIONIST: OK, Mrs Smith. You're in Room 232.
MRS SMITH: Where's that?
RECEPTIONIST: It's on the second floor.
MRS SMITH: Thanks very much.
RECEPTIONIST: Here's your key, Mr Procter.
MR PROCTER: Where's my room?
RECEPTIONIST: It's on the fourth floor. Room 473.
MR PROCTER: Thank you.
RECEPTIONIST: You're welcome.
RECEPTIONIST: You're on the fifth floor, Ms Harriman.
MS HARRIMAN: The fourth floor?
RECEPTIONIST: No, the fifth floor. You're in Room 591.
Here's your key.
MS HARRIMAN: Ah, 591, thank you very much.
RECEPTIONIST: Here's your room key, Miss Collins.
MISS COLLINS: Thank you. Ah, I'm on the seventh floor?
RECEPTIONIST: That's right – Room 740.
MISS COLLINS: That's fine – thanks a lot.
RECEPTIONIST: Here's your key, Mr Charles. You're in
Room 193.
MR CHARLES: Is that on the first floor?
RECEPTIONIST: Yes, it is.
MR CHARLES: Thank you very much.
RECEPTIONIST: You're welcome.

UNIT 3

Lesson A Friends in photographs
Exercise 1
1. A: Is your wife busy?
   B: Yes, she is.
2. A: Is your manager popular?
   B: No, she isn't.
3. A: Are your friends nice?
   B: Yes, they are.
4. A: Are your colleagues nice?
   B: No, they aren't.

Exercise 2
Photo 1
A: Who's this, with the drink?
B: That's Sarah and her husband, Michael. They're our
   friends.
A: Is he old?
B: Erm, Michael's fifty-ish. She's about thirty.
Photo 2
A: Who's that with you?
B: That's my manager - Maria.
A: How old is she?
B: Oh, she's about thirty, I think.
A: You're sixty, she's about thirty, and she's your manager?
B: Mm, but she's a good manager.
Photo 3
A: Who's the man?
B: He's the manager of the coffee shop in the park.
A: And the woman?
B: That's his wife.
A: Oh, yes, I know.
Photo 4
A: Who are they?
B: My colleagues.
A: Aah. Where is it?
B: In Thailand.
A: Oh, yes. Nice elephants. Who's that man?
B: Mm, that's their guide.

Exercise 3
1. LIFT: 31, 32, 33, 34, 35, 36, 37, 38, 39, 40.
   WOMAN: Wow! We're here!
2. MAN: 41, 42, 43, 44, 45, 46, 47, 48, 49, 50 … 51,
   52, 53, 54, 55, 56, 57, 58, 59, 60. That's it!
3. WOMAN: No, John, ssh … Listen, 61, 62, 63, 64, 65,
   66, 67, 68, 69, and … er, yes, Jane? 70.
4. A: … 71, 72, 73, 74, 75, 76, 77, 78, 79, 80, 81, 82, 83,
   84, 85, 86, 87, 88, 89, 90 … 91, 92, 93, 94, 95, 96,
   97, 98, 99, 100. OK?
   B: Yes, thank you.

Lesson B Rings and rooms
Exercise 1
1. A: Is your watch old?
   B: About 30 years old.
   A: Is it still OK?
   B: It's fine. Listen.
2. A: They're beautiful earrings!
   B: Thanks.
   A: Are they special?
   B: Mm, from my husband.
   A: They're really nice.
3. A: Is that a new ring?
   B: Mm, it is.
   A: Is it a bit small?
   B: Mm, it is a bit small, actually, but it's OK on this
   finger.

A: It's nice.
B: Thanks.

Exercise 2
Version 1
A: That ring's nice. Where's it from?
B: Er … it's from Spain, I think.
A: Is this from Japan?
B: No it's from China.
A: It's lovely.
B: Thanks.
A: Where's this from?
B: The ring?
A: Mmm.
B: It's from Ireland.
Version 2
A: That ring's nice. Where's it from? Is it Turkish?
B: No, it's Spanish, I think.
A: Is this Japanese?
B: No, it's Chinese.
A: It's really lovely.
B: Mm. Thanks very much; it is.
A: Where's this from?
B: The ring?
A: Mm.
B: It's Irish, from Dublin.

Lesson C It's our car, thank you
Exercise 1
Picture C
A: Are you lost?
B: Yes, I think we are.
Picture A
A: This is the fourth level.
B: Is it? Our car's on the fifth level.
Picture B
C: Is that our car?
B: I'm not sure.

Lesson D Review and development
Review of Unit 1
Exercise 3
A: How's he today?
B: He's fine.
A: How's she today?
B: She's fine.
A: What's nice at the coffee bar?
B: The coffee.
A: What's good at the restaurant?
B: The tea.

Review of Unit 2
Exercise 1A and 1B
1. A: Is Athens in Greece?
   B: Yes, it is.
2. A: Is London in France?
   B: No, it isn't, it's in England.
3. A: Is Rio in Brazil?
   B: Yes, it is.
4. A: Is Paris in France?
   B: Yes, it is.
5. A: Is New York in London?
   B: No, it isn't, it's in the USA.
6. A: Is Italy in Rome?
   B: No, it isn't. Rome is in Italy.

Exercise 2A
1. A: What's your e-mail address?
   B: It's Maria dot Suarez, that's m-a-r-i-a dot s-u-a-r-
   e-z@v-i-r-t-u-a-l dot n-e-t dot c-o-m dot b-r.
2. A: What's your e-mail address?
   B: It's Angela dot Collins …
   A: Can you spell it, please?
   B: Yes, OK. a-n-g-e-l-a dot c-o-l-l-i-n-s @
   S-i-m-e-x dot d-e-m-o-n dot c-o dot u-k.

Exercise 2B
A: Are you on e-mail?
B: Yes. my address is John, that's j-o-h-n, dot, Smythe,
   that's s-m-y-t-h-e @ unisa (that's u-n-i-s-a) dot
   e-d-u dot a-u.
A: OK, so that's John dot Smythe at unisa dot e-d-u dot
   a-u.
B: Correct.
A: Great. Thanks very much.
B: You're welcome.

UNIT 4

Lesson A Towns
Exercise 2
Version 1
1. Satoshi
INTERVIEWER: Satoshi, is there a cinema in your town?
SATOSHI: Yes, there are three cinemas.
INTERVIEWER: And are there any nightclubs?
SATOSHI: No, there aren't.
INTERVIEWER: Is there a sports centre?

SATOSHI: Yes, there's a big sports centre.
INTERVIEWER: And is there a theatre?
SATOSHI: Yes, there is. It's very old.
2. Raymundo
INTERVIEWER: Raymundo, is there a nightclub in your
town?
RAYMUNDO: Yes. There are four nightclubs in my town.
INTERVIEWER: Four? And is there a cinema or a theatre?
RAYMUNDO: There's a cinema, but there isn't a theatre.
INTERVIEWER: Is there a sports centre?
RAYMUNDO: Yes, there is, there's a small sports centre.
3. Paloma
INTERVIEWER: Hello, Paloma. Is there a cinema in your
town?
PALOMA: Yes, there is, but there isn't a theatre.
INTERVIEWER: Is there a sports centre?
PALOMA: Yes, there's a new sports centre. It's
fantastic!
INTERVIEWER: Are there any nightclubs?
PALOMA: There is one nightclub. It's very good.
Version 2
1. Satoshi
INTERVIEWER: Satoshi, can I ask you about your town?
SATOSHI: Yes, OK.
INTERVIEWER: Thanks. First, is there a cinema in your
town?
SATOSHI: Yes. In fact there are three cinemas.
INTERVIEWER: And are there any nightclubs?
SATOSHI: No, there aren't, unfortunately.
INTERVIEWER: What about a sports centre?
SATOSHI: Yes, there's a really big sports centre. It's
new.
INTERVIEWER: And what about a theatre?
SATOSHI: Yes, there's a theatre. It's a very beautiful
old theatre.
INTERVIEWER: Thanks a lot.
2. Raymundo
INTERVIEWER: Raymundo, can I ask you about your town?
RAYMUNDO: Yes, of course.
INTERVIEWER: Thanks. First of all, is there a nightclub in
your town?
RAYMUNDO: Yes, there are four. Two of them are really
good.
INTERVIEWER: Really? What about cinemas and theatres?
RAYMUNDO: Well, there's a cinema, but I'm afraid there
isn't a theatre.
INTERVIEWER: And is there a sports centre?
RAYMUNDO: Yes, there is, but it's not a very big one,
unfortunately.
INTERVIEWER: Thanks very much.
3. Paloma
INTERVIEWER: Hello, Paloma. Do you think I could ask
you some questions about your town?
PALOMA: Yes, OK.
INTERVIEWER: Is there a cinema in your town?
PALOMA: Yes, there is, but there isn't a theatre.
PALOMA: Yes, there's a new sports centre. It's great!
INTERVIEWER: Are there any nightclubs?
PALOMA: There's one. It's good but it's very
expensive!

Lesson B Large numbers
Exercise 1
Version 1
1. a hundred and eleven
2. two hundred and ninety-four
3. ten thousand and ten
4. three thousand four hundred and fifty-six
5. a hundred and seventy six
6. three hundred and thirty-seven
7. one thousand and one
8. seven hundred and twenty-one
Version 2
1. This is my address – a hundred and eleven Oxford Street.
2. That's two hundred and ninety-four pounds, please.
3. My computer is a ten thousand and ten model.
4. It's three thousand four hundred and fifty-six
   kilometres to Moscow.
5. It's on page a hundred and seventy-six.
6. Is your address three hundred and thirty-seven Station
   Road?
7. It's only one thousand and one dollars.
8. Six hundred and twenty and one hundred and one is
   seven hundred and twenty-one.

Exercise 2
A: Great! Postcards!
B: Yeah, they're from my friends.
A: What's this?
B: That's Topkapı Palace.
A: How old is it?
B: It's over 500 years old.
A: This theatre is fantastic! How old is it?
B: It's the theatre at Epidaurus in Greece. It's over two
   thousand years old.
A: And is this in Australia?
B: Yes, it is – it's the Sydney Opera House. That's about
   30 years old, I think.
A: And what's this?
B: That's Chartres Cathedral in France.

A: Is it very old?
B: It's over 800 years old.
A: Is this Buckingham Palace?
B: No, it isn't. It's the Bank of England.
A: How old is it?
B: It's only about 300 years old.
A: And of course this is the Great Wall of China.
B: That's right. That's over 3,000 years old.
A: Fantastic!

Lesson C In the city

Exercise 2
1. A: Where's the castle?
   B: Here's a map of the city centre. We're here ... in Princes Street ... and there's the castle.
   A: Oh, yes. And there's the cathedral.
   B: They're very near.
   A: Great!
2. A: Excuse me. Where's the university?
   B: It's near the museum. Here.
   A: Thanks very much.
   B: You're welcome.
3. B: How can I help you?
   B: Is there a post office near here?
   A: Yes, there's one in Canongate.
   B: Thanks.

UNIT 5

Lesson A Rooms and things on the walls

Exercise 2
Version 1
A: What have you got on the walls of your living room?
B: Oh I've got one or two things – erm ... family photos, a picture.
A: An old picture?
B: No, very modern, lots of red and yellow and white. Erm ... bookshelves – I've got lots of books.
A: Have you got any clocks?
B: Yes, I've got an old clock on a shelf and ... erm ... one or two letters. Oh, yes and I've got a very nice window in one wall ...
A: Are the walls white?
B: No, they're green and blue.
A: Mm ... nice.

Version 2
A: What have you got on the walls of your living room?
B: Oh I've got one or two things – erm ... family photos, of my mother and father, my son and daughter.
A: And your husband?
B: Oh yes, of course! And erm ... a picture ...
A: An old picture?
B: No, very modern ... it's Spanish, I think, lots of red and yellow and white ...
A: Sounds interesting.
B: Erm ... bookshelves – I've got lots of books.
A: Have you got any clocks?
B: Yes, I've got an old German clock, on a shelf and ... erm, one or two letters from friends. Oh yes and I've got a very nice window in one wall.
A: Are the walls white?
B: No, they're green and blue, very modern.
A: Mm ... nice.

Exercise 3
A: What have you got on the walls of your living room?
B: We've got lots of things.
A: Have you got any photos?
B: Yes, we have.
A: Where are they?
B: They're on a big shelf.
A: How many books have you got?
B: We've got lots.
A: Where are your pictures from?
B: They're Japanese.
A: What colour is your living room?
B: It's white.

Lesson B Big families?

Exercise 2
RUIKO: Where are you from, David?
DAVID: I'm from New Zealand.
RUIKO: Is your family a big one?
DAVID: Mmm ... quite big.
RUIKO: Have you got any brothers and sisters?
DAVID: I've got two brothers and three sisters.
RUIKO: What about your mother and father? Have they got brothers and sisters?
DAVID: Mmm. My mother's got two brothers, but she hasn't got any sisters, and my father's got three sisters and a brother.
RUIKO: That's quite a lot.
DAVID: Mm, What about you, Ruiko?
RUIKO: I'm Japanese. I've got one brother.
DAVID: Have you got any sisters?
RUIKO: No, I haven't. My father's got a sister.
DAVID: What about your mother?
RUIKO: My mother hasn't got any sisters, but she's got a brother.
DAVID: That's a small family.
RUIKO: Mmm, it is.

Lesson C Leaving and feeling

Exercise 1B
Conversation 2
WOMAN: Have you got any envelopes?
RECEPTIONIST: There are some in your room.
WOMAN: What about postcards?
RECEPTIONIST: Sorry, we haven't got any postcards.

Exercise 2B
1. MAN: I'm off to bed now ... I'm really tired.
   WOMAN: OK. Good night, sleep well.
   MAN: Good night. See you in the morning.
   WOMAN: Yeah, see you tomorrow.
2. MAN: See you later, then.
   WOMAN: What time?
   MAN: Oh about seven.
   MAN: OK ... See you.
3. MAN: Are you happy here?
   WOMAN: Mmm, it's a really good flat.
   MAN: Is that one of your pictures?
   WOMAN: Mmm.
   MAN: The colours are lovely.
   WOMAN: Yes, I'm really pleased with it.

Lesson D Review and development

Review of Unit 3

Exercise 1
Listen and cross the numbers. Ready?
A: 62, 45, 82, 99, 28, 90, 60, 57
B: 40, 43, 66, 33, 51

UNIT 6

Lesson A Have a holiday

Exercise 2A
DJ: OK, OK we've got some great holidays for you. Come to Italy, yes, beautiful Italy, and have a great, great time. Fly Qantas, a top airline, and stay at the Sheraton Hotel in wonderful Rome. 500 dollars, yes, 500 dollars. Tell your friends, tell your manager, tell the cat!
Or go to Greece, mmmmm, lovely Athens! Call International Tours today on 0182 55683. See you later!

Exercise 2B
DJ: Come to Brazil for 10 days for 2,000 dollars. Fly Air New Zealand. Stay at the Excelsior Hotel in beautiful Bahia. Call Cheap Travel on 303 67819 today!

Lesson B Tours to cities and countries

Exercise 1
A: My favourite cities are Rome, er, Paris and Prague.
B: Why Prague?
A: Prague is very beautiful – it's got lots of old buildings.
B: Mm, you're right.
A: What about you? What are your favourite cities?
B: Er, New York, er, Istanbul and Sydney.
A: Why Sydney? Is it nice there?
B: Yes, it's a beautiful city and there are lots of good restaurants.

Exercise 2
Version 1
CUSTOMER: Hello.
TRAVEL AGENT: Morning. Can I help you?
CUSTOMER: I'm not sure. Have you got any information on holidays in France?
TRAVEL AGENT: France, erm, hang on, yes ... how about Montpellier?
CUSTOMER: Mmm, Where is it?
TRAVEL AGENT: In the south of France. It's nice.
CUSTOMER: Is it? Mm, er, I'm not sure.
TRAVEL AGENT: OK. Er, how about Greece? Have a look at this brochure of Athens.
CUSTOMER: OK. Thanks. Mm, interesting. What about Oslo?
TRAVEL AGENT: Oh, don't go to Oslo this month – Norway's so cold.
CUSTOMER: Oh, is it? OK. What about Barcelona?
TRAVEL AGENT: One minute, please. John.
JOHN: Yes?
TRAVEL AGENT: Get me that new brochure on Spain and Catalonia, please.
JOHN: OK.
TRAVEL AGENT: Thanks. Here you are ...
CUSTOMER: Thanks. Mmm ... interesting buildings ... mm, nice shops and restaurants.
TRAVEL AGENT: Yes, it's a great city. Take the brochure and read it at home.
CUSTOMER: OK, thanks. Er, what about ...

Version 2
TRAVEL AGENT: Hi, can I help you?
CUSTOMER: Hello. Yes, I'm interested in holidays in Europe.
TRAVEL AGENT: Which countries are you interested in?
CUSTOMER: I'm not sure ... France, I think.
TRAVEL AGENT: What about a short holiday in Montpellier?
CUSTOMER: Mmm, Where is it?
TRAVEL AGENT: In the south of France. It's nice.
CUSTOMER: Have you got a brochure?

TRAVEL AGENT: Montpellier, erm, hang on a minute, erm, yes, here we are. Look at the pictures in this brochure of the South of France.
CUSTOMER: Mm, lots of old buildings, and near the sea.
TRAVEL AGENT: How about Greece? Have a look at this brochure of Athens.
CUSTOMER: Mmm, lovely. Is that the Parthenon?
TRAVEL AGENT: Yeah, that's it.
CUSTOMER: Er, what about Oslo?
TRAVEL AGENT: Oh don't go to Oslo this month – it's so cold in Norway in November.
CUSTOMER: Oh, is it? OK. What about Barcelona, then?
TRAVEL AGENT: Wait a minute, please. John.
JOHN: Uh huh.
TRAVEL AGENT: Get me that new brochure on Spain and Catalonia, please, it's on Jill's table.
JOHN: Yeah, OK.
TRAVEL AGENT: Thanks. Here you are.
CUSTOMER: Mmm, interesting buildings. Look at this cathedral.
TRAVEL AGENT: Yes, it's Gaudi's La Sagrada Familia. Take the brochure and read it at home.
CUSTOMER: That's great. Thanks a lot. Oh, what about Turkey? Have you got ...

Lesson C Hotel rooms and keys

Exercise 3
A: What room are you in?
B: 512.
A: Is it nice?
B: It's OK. The bed's pretty big and there's a telephone on a little old table by the door and a ... er there's a little safe in the wardrobe. There's a lamp by the window and a big old chair under the window. There's an interesting picture by the door, I think. It's a big photo of a king and queen. It's pretty old.

Lesson D Review and development

Review of Unit 4

Exercise 1
OK. What am I bid for this beautiful French chair? About 1899, about 100 years old. Do I hear 200 dollars. 200 dollars. Thank you. 300 dollars? Yes, 300 dollars, thank you, madam. 400? Do I hear 400? It's a beautiful chair from a home in the South of France. 400, thank you, sir. At 400 ... do I hear 500? 500? Thank you, the woman in red. 600? 600? Please? 600 dollars? Yes? Thank you, sir. 700, come on, it's a lovely little chair for a bedroom or living room. 700? Is that a yes? OK, thank you, madam. OK, 800? 800, yes, 800, from the floor, nine hu? ... and 900. Thank you, madam. 1,000 ... do I hear 1,000? A thousand? No? OK at 900 then, 900 it is. 900, once, twice ... sold. Item number 23, a lovely ...

UNIT 7

Lesson A What's the time?

Exercise 1B
Clock 1
A: What's the time?
B: It's six o'clock.
C: It's five past seven.
D: It's ten past eight.

A: What time is it?
B: It's a quarter past nine.
C: It's twenty past ten.
D: It's twenty-five past eleven.

Clock 2
A: Have you got the time?
B: It's half past twelve.
C: It's twenty-five to one.
D: It's twenty to two.

A: What's the time?
B: It's a quarter to three.
C: It's ten to four.
D: It's five to five.

Exercise 1C
1. A: Have you got the time, please?
   B: Yes, it's half past seven.
   A: Is it really?
2. A: Excuse me, what time is it, please?
   B: It's five to one.
   A: Thanks.
3. A: What's the time?
   B: It's one o'clock.
   A: Thanks very much.
4. A: What's the time?
   B: A quarter past four!
   A: Oh no!
5. A: Excuse me, have you got the time, please?
   B: Erm, yes, it's a quarter to eleven.
   A: Thank you.
6. A: What's the time, please?
   B: It's twenty past five.
   A: Twenty past?
   B: Yes.

7. A: Steve, have you got the time?
   B: Yes, five past two.
   A: Thanks a lot.
8. A: Clare, what time is it, please?
   B: It's twenty to ten.

Exercise 2
MAN: I get up at 6 o'clock in the morning.
WOMAN: Really? That's very early. I get up at half past seven, and I have breakfast at 8 o'clock.
MAN: I have breakfast at a quarter to seven and go to work at a quarter past seven. What about you?
WOMAN: I go to work at twenty past eight.
MAN: I get home at eight o'clock.
WOMAN: Really? That's very late. I get home at half past five.

Lesson B Jobs

Exercise 1
1. A: What do you do?
   B: I'm a teacher.
2. A: What's your job?
   B: I'm a doctor.
3. A: What do you do?
   B: I'm a waiter.
4. A: What's your job?
   B: I'm an engineer.
5. A: What do you do?
   B: I'm a businesswoman.
6. A: What's your job?
   B: I'm a shop assistant.

Exercise 2
1. A: What do you do?
   B: I'm a businesswoman.
   A: Oh, really? Where do you work?
   B: I work in two places. I've got offices in New York and London.
2. A: What's your job?
   B: I'm an engineer.
   A: Where do you work?
   B: I work in a small laboratory at home, but I also go to other countries.
3. A: What do you do?
   B: I'm a doctor.
   A: Where do you work?
   B: Most of the time, I work in a large hospital.
4. A: What's your job?
   B: I'm a waiter.
   A: Where do you work?
   B: In a Greek restaurant in the town centre.
   A: Which restaurant?
   B: The Apollo.
   A: Oh, really? That's a good restaurant.
5. A: What do you do?
   B: I'm a shop assistant.
   A: Where do you work?
   B: In a department store in the town.
   A: Which department store?
   B: D & A.
   A: That's interesting. I buy all my clothes there.
6. A: What's your job?
   B: I'm a teacher.
   A: Do you work in a university?
   B: No, I work in a school.

Exercise 3
1. A: What do you do?
   B: I'm a teacher.
   A: What time do you start work?
   B: I start at a quarter to nine in the morning.
   A: And when do you finish?
   B: At half-past four in the afternoon.
2. A: What's your job?
   B: I'm a waiter.
   A: What time do you start work?
   B: At two o'clock in the afternoon.
   A: And when do you finish?
   B: At one o'clock in the morning.
3. A: What's your job?
   B: I'm a shop assistant.
   A: What time do you start work?
   B: I start at half past eight in the morning.
   A: And when do you finish?
   B: I finish at half past five in the afternoon.
4. A: What do you do?
   B: I'm a businesswoman.
   A: What time do you start work?
   B: At about 6 o'clock in the morning.
   A: And when do you finish?
   B: I usually finish at about half past eight in the evening.
5. A: What's your job?
   B: I'm an engineer.
   A: What time do you start work?
   B: Nine o'clock in the morning.
   A: And when do you finish?
   B: I finish at six o'clock in the evening.
6. A: What do you do?
   B: I'm a doctor.
   A: When do you start work?
   B: This week, I start at 9 o'clock in the evening.
   A: And when do you finish?
   B: At 6 o'clock in the morning.

Lesson C Job routines

Exercise 1
CLARE: What do you do, John?
JOHN: I'm a waiter.
CLARE: Do you work in a café?
JOHN: No, I don't. I work in a restaurant.

CLARE: Do you know John?
SUE: No, I don't. What does he do?
CLARE: He's a waiter.
SUE: Does he work in a café?
CLARE: No, he doesn't. He works in a restaurant.

Exercise 2
1. A: John, you're a waiter – what do you do in the restaurant?
   JOHN: Well, I serve customers.
   A: Do you write their bills?
   JOHN: No, I don't. A computer writes the bills.
   A: Do you take their money?
   JOHN: Yes, I do.
2. A: What do you do in the hospital, Doctor Piper?
   DR PIPER: Well, I help people.
   A: Do you take money from them?
   DR PIPER: No, I don't, I write prescriptions.
   A: Do you travel in your job?
   DR PIPER: Yes, I do. I work in three hospitals.
3. A: Dave, you work – what do you do?
   DAVE: Well, I serve customers of course – I help them and I sell them things.
   A: Do you take their money?
   DAVE: Yes, I do.
   A: And do you travel in your job?
   DAVE: No, I don't.
4. A: You're a businesswoman, Caroline. What do you do in your job?
   CAROLINE: I travel a lot. I go to a lot of countries.
   A: Do you sell things?
   CAROLINE: I don't. I buy things for my company.
   A: Do you write letters and phone people?
   CAROLINE: I phone people, but my assistant writes my letters for me.

Lesson D Review and development

Review of Unit 6

Exercise 2
TRAVEL AGENT: Good morning. Come in and sit down.
CUSTOMER: Thanks.
TRAVEL AGENT: Which country are you interested in?
CUSTOMER: Greece. Do you have any information on holidays in Athens?
TRAVEL AGENT: Athens. Yes, I'm sure we have. Hang on. Yes, here you are.
CUSTOMER: Mm – lots of old monuments – and the sea is quite near.
TRAVEL AGENT: How about Italy? Florence is beautiful. Have a look at the brochure.
CUSTOMER: What's it like at this time of the year?
TRAVEL AGENT: It's fantastic!

UNIT 8

Lesson A I like Thai food ... So do I

Exercise 2
WOMAN: I like Chinese food ...
MAN: Me too.
WOMAN: Erm, I like French food.
MAN: So do I, especially lovely, fresh French bread.
WOMAN: Mm, lovely. Erm, I like Thai food, Indian food ...
MAN: So do I. We eat a lot of spicy food at home.
WOMAN: Uhuh. And I like pizza. Is that Italian food?
MAN: Yes, but it's also international.
WOMAN: Mmm, it is ... well I like traditional pizza ...
MAN: Mmm, me too – good pizza, with a nice fresh salad ...

Exercise 3
Version 1
TEACHER: Stefan, do you like Mexican food?
STEFAN: No, I don't, it's very hot.
TEACHER: Do you like Indian or Thai food?
STEFAN: No, I don't.
TEACHER: What about Italian? Do you like Italian food?
STEFAN: Yes, I do. It's my favourite. And there are lots of Italian restaurants near my home. What about you? Do you like Italian food?
TEACHER: No, I don't. I like hot food. I like Thai food; it's spicy and very nice.

Version 2
TEACHER: Stefan, does your sister like Mexican food?
STEFAN: No, she doesn't, it's very hot.
TEACHER: Does she like Indian or Thai food?
STEFAN: No, she doesn't.
TEACHER: What about Chinese? Does she like Chinese food?
STEFAN: Yes, she does. It's her favourite. And there are lots of Chinese restaurants near her home. What about your sister? Does she like Chinese food?
TEACHER: I haven't got a sister.

STEFAN: Your brother then.
TEACHER: No, he likes spicy food. He likes Indian food very much. His wife's from India.
STEFAN: Really?
TEACHER: Mmm, from Bombay, she's an actress.
STEFAN: Really?
TEACHER: Mmm.

Lesson B Sandwiches – the international food

Exercise 2
A: Do you like coffee?
B: Good coffee, yes, but I don't like coffee with sugar. It's awful.
A: What about your husband?
B: Oh, he doesn't like coffee, but he loves tea – tea at eight, nine, ten, eleven – he likes tea all the time!
A: Really?
B: Mm, and he likes it with lots of sugar. It's not good!
C: Do you like sandwiches?
D: We don't eat sandwiches much in our country but we like sandwiches in England.
C: Do you like simple sandwiches or sandwiches with lots of different things inside?
D: I like simple sandwiches – ham on fresh bread for example, but my wife likes sandwiches with different things in. She likes meat, salad and fruit jam sandwiches, for example.
C: Really?
D: Mm, our friends in England make lots of interesting sandwiches for her. But we don't like the sandwiches in some of the coffee shops: the bread isn't very nice.

Lesson C Conversations and courses

Exercise 2A
1. Good evening, Smith's restaurant.
2. Hello, Schmidt's restaurant.
3. Hello, Smee's restaurant, can I help you?

Exercise 2B
A: Is that Smith's?
B: Sorry? What? It's a bad line.
A: Is that Smith's restaurant?
B: I'm sorry ... is that who?
A: Smith's.
B: What number do you want?
A: 288 40212.
B: You've got the wrong number. This is 288 40202.
A: Oh, I'm sorry.
B: That's OK, bye.

Exercise 2C
A: Is that Smith's?
B: I'm sorry?
A: Is that Smith's restaurant?
B: What number do you want?
A: 288 40212.
B: I think you've got the wrong number. This is 288 40202.
A: Oh, I'm sorry.
B: That's OK, bye.

Exercise 3A
January February March April May June July August October September November December

Exercise 3B
LUDMILA: Hi, I'm Ludmila.
INTERVIEWER: Oh, hello, thanks for coming. I've got one or two questions about your course, OK?
LUDMILA: Yes, fine.
INTERVIEWER: OK. How long is your English course?
LUDMILA: Er, three months – July, August and September.
INTERVIEWER: How many weeks is that?
LUDMILA: Er, 12 weeks, I think, yeah, 12.
INTERVIEWER: How many hours a week are you in class?
LUDMILA: Four hours per week.
INTERVIEWER: What days and times?
LUDMILA: Tuesday and Thursday from 7 till 9.
INTERVIEWER: Seven till 9 p.m.?
LUDMILA: Yes, 7 till 9 in the evening after work.
INTERVIEWER: What week of your course is this week?
LUDMILA: Week ten ... mm, the tenth week.
INTERVIEWER: And is the course OK?
LUDMILA: Yes, it's fine, but I don't like listening, it's very fast for me.
INTERVIEWER: OK ... well, thanks, Ludmila.
LUDMILA: You're welcome.

Quick Check Exercise C
MAN: Hi, is John there?
WOMAN: Sorry, who do you want to speak to?
MAN: John.
WOMAN: John who?
MAN: John Smith.
WOMAN: Sorry, you've got the wrong number.
MAN: I'm sorry, bye.
WOMAN: Bye.

UNIT 9

Lesson A Shopping

Exercise 2A
1. MAN: Excuse me.
   ASSISTANT: Yes.
   MAN: Have you got a T-shirt with *I love Australia* on it?
   ASSISTANT: Yes, we have. What colour would you like?
   MAN: Have you got a dark blue T-shirt?
   ASSISTANT: Yes, we have.
2. ASSISTANT: Good morning.
   WOMAN: Hi. Can I have this necklace, please?
   ASSISTANT: Yes, of course. Is it a present?
   WOMAN: Yes, it is.
3. ASSISTANT: Hello, can I help you?
   MAN: Yes, I'd like a small television, please.
   ASSISTANT: This one?
   MAN: No, a very small one – the size of a camera.
   ASSISTANT: Ah, yes. What colour would you like?
   MAN: Have you got black?
   ASSISTANT: Yes, we've got black, white or red.
4. WOMAN: Hi. Can I have these CDs, please?
   ASSISTANT: Thank you.
   WOMAN: And have you got the new Phil Collins CD?
   ASSISTANT: Yes, we have.
   WOMAN: Can I have two, please?
5. ASSISTANT: Good morning. Can I help you?
   MAN: Yes, I'd like a teddy bear, please.
   ASSISTANT: Yes, of course. A big one or a small one?
   MAN: Oh, not too big.

Exercise 2C
1. MAN: Excuse me.
   ASSISTANT: Yes.
   MAN: Have you got a T-shirt with I love Australia on it?
   ASSISTANT: Yes, we have. What colour would you like?
   MAN: Have you got a dark blue T-shirt?
   ASSISTANT: Yes, we have.
   MAN: Good.
   ASSISTANT: And size? Large, medium or small?
   MAN: Small, please – it's for my wife.
2. ASSISTANT: Good morning.
   WOMAN: Hi. Can I have this necklace, please?
   ASSISTANT: Yes, of course. Is it a present?
   WOMAN: Yes, it is.
   ASSISTANT: Who's it for?
   WOMAN: It's a souvenir for my daughter.
3. ASSISTANT: Hello, can I help you?
   MAN: Yes, I'd like a small television, please.
   ASSISTANT: This one?
   MAN: No, a very small one – the size of a camera.
   ASSISTANT: Ah, yes. What colour would you like?
   MAN: Have you got black?
   ASSISTANT: Yes, we've got black, white or red.
   MAN: White, please. It's a present for my girlfriend.
4. WOMAN: Hi. Can I have these CDs, please?
   ASSISTANT: Thank you.
   WOMAN: And have you got the new Phil Collins CD?
   ASSISTANT: Yes, we have.
   WOMAN: Can I have two, please? One for my sister and one for my husband. It's his birthday tomorrow.
5. ASSISTANT: Good morning. Can I help you?
   MAN: Yes, I'd like a teddy bear, please.
   ASSISTANT: Yes, of course. A big one or a small one?
   MAN: Oh, not too big. It's for my grandson – he's only ten weeks old.

Lesson B Money matters

Exercise 1
1. That's seven hundred and fifty yen.
2. 40,000 lire, please.
3. Ninety pounds? That's really expensive!
4. They're 300 drachma each.
5. That's about 200 pesetas.
6. It's seventeen deutschmarks.
7. Hmm. eighty dollars – that's quite cheap.
8. I think it's eighteen dollars.

Exercise 2A
1. A: Good holiday?
   B: Yeah, wonderful. Italian people are so friendly.
   A: I like your shoes.
   B: They're from Rome.
2. A: Hi.
   B: Jill! Come in.
   A: How was America?
   B: Fantastic!
   A: And New York?
   B: Busy!
   A: Hey, I like the painting! It's very modern.
   B: That's from New York.
3. A: Paul! You're back!
   B: Hi.
   A: Nice time in England?
   B: Yes, great.
   A: And the weather?
   B: Not so good.
   A: I like your umbrella.
   B: Thanks – it's from London.

4. A: I love your sunglasses.
   B: They're Spanish.
   A: Oh yeah. How was the holiday?
   B: Wonderful.

Exercise 2B
1. A: Hello, can I help?
   B: Yes, how much is that painting?
   A: The large, modern one?
   B: Yes.
   A: It's two hundred dollars.
   B: That's very cheap.
2. A: How much are these sunglasses, please?
   B: They're eight hundred pesetas.
   A: That's not bad and they're very nice.
3. A: I really like these shoes. How much are they?
   B: They're two hundred thousand lire.
   A: Phew! That's very expensive.
   B: They're Gucci shoes.
4. A: How much is this umbrella?
   B: This week it's fifteen pounds.
   A: That's cheap for a large umbrella.

Lesson C Telephone shopping

Exercise 2
A: Hello. Telephone sales. Can I help you?
B: Oh yes, hello. I'd like some things from the catalogue.
A: Yes, what would you like?
B: The desk fax.
A: What's the code number?
B: It's DFX–33.
A: DFX–33. That's £284. Do you want black or green?
B: Green, please.
A: Green. Yes?
B: And the night watch. That's WWN2.
A: The night watch. Yes. That's £29.99. Anything else?
B: No, that's all thanks.
A: Right. That's the desk fax and the night watch. That's £313.99. How do you want to pay?
B: Credit card. Is that OK?
A: Fine. What's your card number, please?
B: 5647 2165 4583 2409.
A: And your name and address, please.
B: Paul North ...
A: Paul North.
B: 17, London Road, Liverpool.
A: Thank you, Mr North.

UNIT 10

Lesson A Work and clothes

Exercise 2
1. INTERVIEWER: Mark, what do you wear at the weekend?
   MARK: I usually wear trousers – not jeans – and a shirt. I sometimes wear a pullover.
   INTERVIEWER: Do you wear a hat?
   MARK: No, I don't.
2. INTERVIEWER: Monica, what do you wear at the weekend?
   MONICA: Mmm, I usually wear just jeans and a sweatshirt. And sandals – I love my sandals.
3. INTERVIEWER: Angela, what do you wear at the weekend?
   ANGELA: Well, I love long dresses, especially for parties. My favourite dress is black at the moment. And at discos, I usually wear a mini-skirt and a bright blouse.
4. INTERVIEWER: What do you wear at the weekend, Pierre?
   PIERRE: Shorts and a T-shirt. On the beach I sometimes wear a baseball cap and sunglasses.

Lesson B Possessions

Exercise 3
OK here are the answers: Mouth A is Nelson Mandela. Mouth B is Pope John Paul II. Mouth C is Tiger Woods. Mouth D is Martina Hingis. Mouth E is Cindy Crawford. Mouth F is John Lennon. How many have you got right?

Lesson C It's lovely

Exercise 1
1. BOY: Dad, can I have some new shoes?
   FATHER: Yes, OK.
   BOY: I like the black shoes in the window.
   FATHER: No, I'm sorry, they're too expensive.
2. GIRL: Do you like my new jeans, Mark?
   BOY: They're OK.
   GIRL: What do you think of the colour?
   BOY: It's lovely. Yellow really suits you.
   GIRL: So, what's the problem?
   BOY: They're too bright. Your mum doesn't like bright clothes.
3. ASSISTANT: Hello, can I help you?
   CUSTOMER: Yes, I'd like to change this jacket.
   ASSISTANT: What's the problem?
   CUSTOMER: It's too big for me.

4. MOTHER: That skirt is very short.
   GIRL: It's a mini-skirt, Mum. Mini-skirts are always short.
   MOTHER: But it doesn't suit you. It's too short for you.

Exercise 3
I'm on holiday in Florida. I love America, but there are problems. There is a nightclub near the hotel – the music is too loud. And I don't like the weather. It's too hot for me. Here's a photo of me in my holiday clothes. Do you like my T-shirt? And what about my hat? Do you think it's too big for me? I think it's fantastic! Don't worry, I only wear it on the beach.
See you next week.
Love,
Paula

UNIT 11

Lesson A You've got the job!

Exercise 2
Version 1
A: OK ... first question. Can you write good business letters?
B: Mm, yes, I can.
A: OK. Er, what about reports? Can you write a good report?
B: Mm, I can. I like writing.
A: Do you like people?
B: Yes, of course I like people ... I've got no problem with people from any country.
A: Right. Can you talk to people on the phone?
B: Oh, yes, I can talk on the phone. I'm good.
A: What about computers? Can you use computers?
B: No, I can't. I don't like computers.
Version 2
A: OK ... first question. Can you write good business letters?
B: Mm, yes, I can. I can write any sort of letter. I'm a good writer because I write a lot.
A: OK. Erm, what about reports? Can you write a good report?
B: Mm, I can. I'm a good writer ... letters, reports, I can write anything.
A: Do you like people?
B: Yes, of course I like people. I've got no problem with people from any country, and I can speak French and Italian.
A: Right. Can you talk to people on the phone?
B: Oh, yes, I can talk on the phone. I'm good with people and they like me ... I think.
A: What about computers? Can you use computers?
B: No, I can't, I'm afraid. I don't like computers because I've got a bad back.

Lesson B Work in other countries

Exercise 3
A: In Australia, in my profession, you see an advert in a newspaper and you telephone the company to talk about the job and ask for an application form. Your job interview is very important. The interview can be with four or five people. You talk about salary at the interview because the salary is not in the advert.
INTERVIEWER: When do you hear about the job?
A: You wait about two weeks or so and you get a letter. Some people wait a long time because they haven't got the job and the company forgets to write!
B: In my profession in Ecuador, you see a job advertisement in the newspaper and you write for an application form. You don't phone the company. You send a photo with your application form. For some jobs there isn't an interview, but for jobs with private companies there is an interview, maybe with two people. You don't talk about salary at the interview because the salary is in the advertisement, so you know the money you can get.
INTERVIEWER: When do you hear about the job?
B: You get a letter after about one week. Some people wait a long time because the company doesn't write to everyone.

Lesson C Excuses, excuses

Exercise 3
1. CARLOS: Hi, Sofia.
   SOFIA: Hi.
   CARLOS: Can you come to dinner?
   SOFIA: When?
   CARLOS: On Sunday.
   SOFIA: I'm sorry, Carlos, but it's Linda's birthday on Sunday. She's three.
   CARLOS: Mmm. OK.
   SOFIA: Phone Sven. Perhaps he's free.
   CARLOS: OK. Thanks, bye.

TAPESCRIPTS

2. CARLOS: Sven, hi, it's Carlos. How are you?
 SVEN: Fine.
 CARLOS: Look can you come to dinner on Sunday?
 SVEN: On Sunday?
 CARLOS: Mmm.
 SVEN: I'm sorry, Carlos. My mother is ill ... and I'm very busy.
 CARLOS: Oh, I'm sorry about your mother.
 SVEN: What about Maria? Maybe she can go.
 CARLOS: Mmm, that's an idea. Thanks. Bye.
3. CARLOS: Maria, hi, how are you?
 MARIA: Fine, thanks, Carlos, how about you?
 CARLOS: Oh, I'm OK. Can you come for dinner on Sunday?
 MARIA: Oh, I'm very busy.
 CARLOS: Oh, really?
 MARIA: Yes. My son's at home from university. I'm really tired and I've got this report to finish ... for you!
 CARLOS: Oh, yes. Erm, what about Monday evening?

Lesson D Review and development
Review of Unit 9
Exercise 3B
1. phone; code; know
2. you; do; school
3. cost; boss; clock
4. your; all; floor
5. town; how; thousand

Review of Unit 10
Exercise 2
1. This is my office.
2. Do you like my new yellow jeans?
3. Where's the hotel?
4. Send me a postcard.
5. That train is too early.
6. Say it again, please.
7. The weather is terrible.
8. Can you repeat that, please?

UNIT 12

Lesson A Making plans
Exercise 2A
SATOSHI: Do you like our English course?
MAYUMI: Yes, I do. It's very good and everyone's really friendly.
SATOSHI: When does it finish? Do you know?
MAYUMI: At the end of next week.
SATOSHI: Let's have a goodbye party.
MAYUMI: Great idea!

Exercise 2B
SATOSHI: Do you like our English course?
MAYUMI: Yes, I do. It's very good and everyone's really friendly.
SATOSHI: When does it finish? Do you know?
MAYUMI: At the end of next week.
SATOSHI: Let's have a goodbye party.
MAYUMI: Great idea! Where?
SATOSHI: Our flat?
MAYUMI: No, it's too small. What about the beach?
SATOSHI: The beach is too cold at night.
MAYUMI: A hotel with a disco?
SATOSHI: That's a good idea. What about the New York Hotel? That's got a good disco.
MAYUMI: That sounds great. And when, Saturday?
SATOSHI: No, people often do other things on Saturdays. Let's have it on Friday.
MAYUMI: OK. Next Friday then – at ten o'clock?
SATOSHI: No, ten o'clock's too late. What about nine?
MAYUMI: Fine. So that's next Friday at nine o'clock. Let's write the invitations.

Lesson B Invitations
Exercise 2A
1. Cecile
CECILE: Hello.
SATOSHI: Hi, Cecile, it's Satoshi.
CECILE: Satoshi. How are you?
SATOSHI: I'm fine. Listen, can you come to our party?
CECILE: Yes, I can.
SATOSHI: Can you bring a friend?
CECILE: Yes, he's called Pascal – he's French.
2. John
A: Hello.
SATOSHI: Hello. Can I speak to John, please?
A: Yes, of course. One moment.
JOHN: Hello, this is John.
SATOSHI: John, this is Satoshi. Can you come to the party next Friday?
JOHN: No, I can't. Sorry.
SATOSHI: Don't worry. That's OK.
JOHN: Have a good time.

3. Peter
PETER: Hello.
MAYUMI: Hi, Peter, it's Mayumi.
PETER: Mayumi! How are you?
MAYUMI: I'm fine. Listen, can you come to our party on Friday?
PETER: I'm not sure. I'm very busy this week. Perhaps.
4. Maria
MARIA: Hello.
SATOSHI: Is that Maria?
MARIA: Yes, it is, who's that?
SATOSHI: It's Satoshi from school.
MARIA: I'm sorry, I can't come to your party on Saturday.
SATOSHI: It isn't on Saturday. It's on Friday.
MARIA: Oh, great! I can come on Friday.
SATOSHI: Wonderful! Can you bring a friend?
MARIA: Yes, of course. Manuel – he's my husband.
SATOSHI: Oh, good.
MARIA: See you on Friday.
SATOSHI: OK. Thanks. Bye.
5. Lucy
LUCY: Hello.
MAYUMI: Hi, Lucy – it's Mayumi.
LUCY: Oh, hi.
MAYUMI: Can you come to the party on Friday?
LUCY: Probably. I don't really know.
MAYUMI: That's OK.
LUCY: I want to come, but my father is not very well.
MAYUMI: I'm sorry. Try to come.
LUCY: OK.

Exercise 2B
1. John
A: Hello.
SATOSHI: Hello. Can I speak to John, please?
A: Yes, of course. One moment.
JOHN: Hello, this is John.
SATOSHI: John, this is Satoshi. Can you come to the party next Friday?
JOHN: No, I can't. Sorry.
SATOSHI: Oh, that's a pity.
2. Peter
PETER: Peter here.
MAYUMI: Hi, Peter, it's Mayumi.
PETER: Mayumi! How are you?
MAYUMI: I'm fine. Listen, can you come to our party on Friday?
PETER: I'm not sure. I'm very busy this week. Perhaps.
3. Lucy
LUCY: Hello.
MAYUMI: Hi, Lucy – it's Mayumi.
LUCY: Oh, hi.
MAYUMI: Can you come to the party on Friday?
LUCY: I don't really know. Probably.

Lesson C The party
Exercise 1.
Conversation 1
CECILE: Hi, Raymundo. How are you?
RAYMUNDO: I'm fine, thanks. And you?
CECILE: OK. This is my friend, Pascal.
RAYMUNDO: Pleased to meet you. This is Karen. She's my girlfriend.
CECILE: Hi. Where are you from?
KAREN: I'm from Mexico. Are you from France, Pascal?
PASCAL: Yes, I am. I'm from Normandy.
KAREN: Normandy. That's famous for cheese, isn't it?
PASCAL: That's right.
KAREN: What do you do there?
PASCAL: I buy all the cheese for a big French supermarket.
Conversation 2
MAYUMI: Hi, Lucy, I'm pleased you're here.
LUCY: It's nice to be here.
MAYUMI: How's your father?
LUCY: He's OK now, thanks. Oh, Mayumi, this is Tran.
MAYUMI: Hi. Where are you from?
TRAN: I'm from Vietnam. It's a great party.
MAYUMI: Thanks. Do you like the music?
TRAN: Yes, what is it?
MAYUMI: It's Japanese.
LUCY: It's very interesting. It's very different from American or European music. But I like it a lot.
TRAN: Me too.
Conversation 3
PETER: Hi.
SATOSHI: Hello, Peter. What a surprise!
PETER: It's a really nice party.
SATOSHI: Thanks.
PETER: The food looks fantastic.
SATOSHI: There's something from everyone's country. Look this is our Japanese food.
PETER: What's this?
SATOSHI: That's French – from Cecile and Pascal. I think it's chicken in red wine.
PETER: It looks wonderful. I haven't got anything, I'm afraid.
SATOSHI: That's OK. Everyone knows you're too busy this week.

Conversation 4
MARIA: Hi, Eva.
EVA: Hi. It's a great party, isn't it?
MARIA: Yeah. Eva, this is my husband, Manuel. He's Spanish.
EVA: Pleased to meet you, Manuel. And this is my best friend, Nicole from Holland. She's here on holiday.
MANUEL: Where are you from in Holland?
NICOLE: I'm from Rotterdam, but I live in Washington now.
MARIA: What do you do there?
NICOLE: I'm a journalist for a Dutch newspaper.
MANUEL: Do you like the States?
NICOLE: Yes, I do. It's a really interesting place, but I would like to go back to Holland.
MARIA: Really?
NICOLE: Yes, I want to have children soon.

Lesson D Review and development
Review of Unit 11
Exercise 1A
1. A: Does she go to work on Saturdays?
 B: No, I don't think so.
2. A: Can he go to Barcelona this morning?
 B: No, he can't, there's a meeting at 10.
 A: Oh, OK.
3. A: Do they come from Hungary?
 B: Yes, from Tblisi.
4. A: Can she phone Monika at nine, please?
 B: I think so. Mmm, that's fine.
 A: Thanks. Bye.
5. A: Does he like the new job?
 B: Mm, very much.
 A: That's good.
6. A: Does she like Italian food?
 B: Italian? I don't know. I think so.

Exercise 1B
1. A: Can he go to Barcelona?
 B: No, he can't.
2. A: Can she phone Monika at nine?
 B: Yes, she can.

Unit 3, Lesson B, Exercise 2
The ring is from Sudan.
The earrings are from Tahiti.

ACKNOWLEDGEMENTS

Authors' acknowledgements

We would like to thank the other series authors Ruth Gairns, Stuart Redman and Joanne Collie for their professionalism and continuing support as the *True to Life* series grows. Special thanks to Joanne Collie for her valuable feedback on early drafts of this material.

At Cambridge University Press our special thanks go to our commissioning editor, Kate Boyce, who has been a patient, courteous, and constant professional guide throughout the writing, feedback, revision and production process. To our editor, Helena Gomm, we are grateful for her tireless excellence in ensuring economy, consistency and accuracy. We are grateful also to Frances Amrani for editing the Teacher's Book, to Martin Williamson of Prolingua Productions and the staff at Studio AVP for producing the recordings, and to the design team, Samantha Dumiak and Gecko Limited.

Stephen Slater is grateful to his family for their patience and to the family dog for her unconditional enthusiasm for life, which has transferred valuable, positive energy to him when he really needed it.

The authors and publishers would like to thank the following individuals and institutions for their help in testing the material and for the invaluable feedback which they provided:
Laura Renart, T. S. Eliot Institute, Buenos Aires, Argentina; Pat MacRitchie, Hawthorn English Language Centre, Victoria, Australia; Judy D'All, Centre d'Anglais d'Angers, Angers, France; Don Ward, Centre d'Étude des Langues, Évry Cedex, France; Miriam Zeh-Glöckler, Sprachwerkstatt Glöckler, Leipzig, Germany; Kerry Flanagan, Regent Italia, Milan, Italy; Suzanne Wragge, Buckingham School, Rome, Italy; Michelle Hug, Rothrist, Switzerland; Canan O'Flynn, Bilgi University, Istanbul, Turkey.

The authors and publishers are grateful to the following illustrators and photographic sources:
Illustrators: David Axtell: pp. 5 *b*, 9 *b*, 36, 76; Kathy Baxendale: pp. 7, 26, 46, 63; Lee Ebrell: pp. 8, 16, 20, 22, 25, 39, 41, 39, 58 *t*; Martin Fish: pp. 9 *tr*, 38, 43, 66, 80 *t*, 81, 83 *t*, 90, 98; Steve Lach: pp. 6, 24, 62, 97; Mark McLaughlin: pp. 5 *t*, 37, 52, 68, 84, 87; Tracy Rich: pp. 14, 23, 30, 40, 46, 60, 70, 71, 83 *b*; Martin Sanders: pp. 28, 32, 47, 58 *b*; Jamie Sneddon: pp. 7, 8, 9, 11, 15, 16, 21, 23, 25, 26, 28, 31, 32, 34, 35, 40, 41, 43, 46, 51, 65, 75, 81, 84, 85, 88, 96, 103; Kath Walker: pp. 44, 64, 80 *b*, 82, 88, 89, 100, 101, 102, 104, 105; Rosemary Woods: p. 29.

Photographic sources: Action-Plus Photographic: p. 78 (racer); Peter Adams: p. 85 (nurse); Tick Ahearn: p. 13 (all except Statue of Liberty & World Trade Center); Ancient Art & Architecture Collection: p. 30 *br* (G. T. Garvey); Paul Beard: pp. 38, 50; The Bell Educational Trust: p. 19 *cl*; Bord Failte – Irish Tourist Board: p. 33 *b* (Bryan Lynch); Collections: p. 85 (engineer: R. J. Davis); E. T. Archive: p. 7 *c*; Malcolm Fife: p. 32; Leslie Garland: p. 44 *r*; Hulton Getty Collection: p. 7 *b*; courtesy of ICI: p. 53 *bc*; Image Bank: p. 4 *c* (Steve Niedorf); Joel Photography: p. 30 *bcl*; Melvyn P. Lawes: p. 30 *tr*; Life File: pp. 12 *br*, 35 *c* (Emma Lee), 12 *tr*, 35 *br* (Jeremy Hoare), 13 (Statue of Liberty: Su Davies), 19 *cr* (Mike Maidment), 31 *bl* (Andrew Ward), 33 *l* (Arthur Jumper), 33 *t* (Nigel Shuttleworth), 37 *t* (Barry Mayes), 78 (nun: Paul Fisher); Nigel Luckhurst: pp. 21 *bl*, *br*, 22 *t* (jewellery courtesy of Cellini, Cambridge), 21 *bc*, 22 *cl*, *cr*, *br*, *bl*; Popperfoto: pp. 78 (UN), 79 (Mandela, Pope, Lennon), 79 (Reuters: Woods, Hingis, Crawford); David Simson: pp. 4 (all except *c*), 7 *t*, 8, 10, 11, 12 *tl*, *bl*, 13 (World Trade Center), 14, 15, 16, 17, 19 *l*, *r*, 20, 21 *tl*, *tr*, 25, 30 *tl*, *bl*, *bcr*, 31 *t*, *br*, *bc*; 35 *t*, *bl*, 37 *bl*, *br*, 39, 40, 42 *r*, 44 *l*, 48, 49, 51, 53 (all except *bc*); 54, 55, 56, 57, 61, 63, 64, 70, 73, 75, 78 *l*, 78 (fireman), 78 *r*, 81, 85 (all except doctor, nurse, engineer), 86, 88, 92, 95; Mike Wyndham Picture Collection: p. 78 (nurse), 85 (doctor).

t = top, *b* = bottom, *c* = centre, *l* = left, *r* = right

Design and production by Gecko Ltd, Bicester, Oxon.
Picture research by Callie Kendall.
Sound recordings by Martin Williamson, Prolingua Productions, at Studio AVP, London.

The authors and publishers are grateful to the following for permission to reproduce photographs on the cover:
Life File: *tl* (Andrew Ward); *tc* (Graham Burns), *tr*, *bl* (Emma Lee), *bc* (Barry Mayes), *br* (Dave Thompson).